IN THE

photographs and illustrations by *Art Wolfe*

RESENCE OF

text by *Gregory McNamee*

WOLVES

CROWN PUBLISHERS, INC., NEW YORK

Photographs copyright © 1995 by Art Wolfe

Text copyright © 1995 by Gregory McNamee

Published by Crown Publishers, Inc., 201 East 50th Street, New York, New York 10022. Member of the Crown Publishing Group.

Random House, Inc., New York, Toronto, London, Sydney, Auckland

CROWN is a trademark of Crown Publishers, Inc.

Manufactured in Japan

Design by Lauren Dong

Library of Congress Cataloging-in-Publication Data
Wolfe, Art.
  In the presence of wolves / photographs by Art Wolfe; text compiled by and with an introduction by Gregory McNamee.—1st ed.
  Includes index.
   1. Wolves.   2. Wolves—Pictorial works.   I. McNamee, Gregory.
II. Title.
QL737.C22W6456   1995
599.74'442—dc20   94-37316
                                                                CIP

ISBN 0-517-79978-2

10 9 8 7 6 5 4 3 2 1

First Edition

in the presence of Wolves

A WORD FROM THE PHOTOGRAPHER

Throughout recorded history the wolf has attained a prominent position in mythology, ceremony, and folklore. The wolf's likeness has been chiseled into the cave walls of primeval Europe and painted on the canvases of contemporary illustrators. The wolf gave rise to the legends of werewolves, and the cunning villain in "Little Red Riding Hood." The wolf's reputation as the evil creature that lurks in the shadows awaiting the unwary is so ingrained in our consciousness, even today I am asked how I protect myself when traveling in wolf country.

Humankind's fascination with the wolf, like that with the shark, tiger, and grizzly, is borne as much from its secretive behavior as from its hunting prowess. Our instinctual response to the wolf is a sense of both fear and envy—homage from one excellent predator to another.

From the onset of my career, I have held a special interest in the wolf. I have spent countless hours peering through spotting scopes and binoculars; from the Arctic plains of Alaska's North Slope to the deep-cut valleys of the Rocky Mountains, I have looked for what, at times, seems like a mythical creature. Like other photographers, my sightings and ulti-

mate photographs have been hard-earned ones. Through the years, I have had my share of memorable encounters, and I have come to know the animal as one to admire and respect, rather than a beast to loathe and fear.

One year I helicoptered into a remote den site in the mountains west of Tok Junction, near the Alaska-Canada border. A biologist had located the den the previous year and agreed to guide me to it. Upon our arrival it looked deserted. Wolves often alternate den sites from year to year, allowing the empty den to clear of parasites. I decided to remain 48 hours while the pilot and biologist returned to Tok. Before they left, they completely entombed me and my tent in a dense shroud of moss and shrubs, leaving only my 800mm telephoto slightly protruding. My blind was 50 yards from the den at an excellent vantage point if anything passed by. The only light to penetrate the buried tent came by way of my camera's viewfinder. It was dark, dank, and claustrophobic. I had a sleeping bag, flashlight, book, candy bars, and water.

For the first 20 hours I peered through my viewfinder at 10-minute intervals until I was completely convinced that I was the only breathing

During June of 1994, a friend and I traveled to Alaska's Denali National Park. We were specifically hoping to catch a glimpse of a wolf, and with a little luck we would photograph some behavior.

Upon our arrival we ran into some photographers who had been working in the park prior to our arrival. They offered absolutely no encouragement; apparently, wolf sightings were very few and far between. In addition, the weather was dismal. There were very few days in that month when it had not been raining. Another factor that seemed to work against us was that we had scheduled only four days to work within the park.

The next morning, we traveled well into the park. We were driving down toward the Toklat River, one of the major rivers that flows out of the Alaska Range through the park. We had rounded the bend, fully $2^1/_2$ miles from the river itself, when I caught a glimpse of a very small dot moving up the river plain. I grabbed my binoculars and focused in on a bull caribou running as though it was being pursued by a predator—a grizzly or perhaps a wolf. We both scanned eagerly for what was chasing the caribou, and discovered, a full half mile behind in pursuit, a wolf! At this we quickly accelerated down the road until we came to a bridge crossing the river. By now we had lost sight of both animals. As we got out of the car and scanned the river valley leading into the wilderness, we could not see a thing. We drove farther up the road to a better viewpoint and scanned the upper reaches of the Toklat. At the bend of the river, we spotted the caribou standing defiantly on a rocky bar in the middle of the river. Upon closer inspec-

organism within miles of the den. At the 24-hour mark, I fell asleep. When I awoke, I sleepily gazed into my viewfinder and was shocked to see four fuzzy little pups playing at the den entrance. To my utter joy, they were completely unaware of my presence. For the following five hours I remained silently mesmerized by the amazing array of behavior unfolding before me. From tail-biting, to tag, to synchronized howling, those pups put on quite a show. Meanwhile, I was able to get a few photographs of an adult as it approached the den. Unfortunately, whenever the pups interacted with the adult, it was out of my view. I was frustrated, but could do nothing but wait for them to reappear.

Eventually I heard the distant whir of the helicopter, and the wolves sunk back into the forest. I had a tough time convincing the skeptical biologist of what I had witnessed.

tion we noticed the gray wolf circling the caribou at an approximate range of three to four feet—just out of reach of hooves and antlers. We quickly discussed the feasibility of getting in close enough to the encounter to catch it on film. We decided we had nothing to lose and packed up our gear, then headed out across the tundra, crossing many small riverlets and trekking through very dense tundra foliage and willow thickets.

At the point where we last saw the caribou, we ascended a small hillock and surveyed the surrounding countryside. To our great surprise, the caribou bull was sitting on the river bar with absolutely no wolf in sight. We sat down to catch our breath and for 40 minutes scanned the area, trying to find the wolf. At this point we determined that if the caribou was confident enough to put itself in such a vulnerable position, surely the wolf was nowhere in the immediate vicinity.

Discouraged and disappointed, we decided to eat our lunch, pack up, and return to our vehicle. As soon as we stood up and started to leave, the caribou arose. As soon as its prey moved, the wolf appeared from nowhere. Apparently it had been curled up, sleeping, about 50 yards away, completely camouflaged against the gray rocks of the river bar. The caribou bolted up the bar with the wolf in hot pursuit. Our response was to follow at a respectful distance of about 300 feet. Keeping up with the chase was difficult enough. The wolf soon caught up to the bull and started nipping at its heels, testing the caribou's strength. The caribou, in fear for its very life, stopped abruptly, whirling its head around, trying to gore the wolf with its antlers.

I filmed this encounter, feeding 12 rolls of film through my camera, and using a 800mm telephoto lens and 2 tripods. It was very late in the

afternoon, and the clouds were heavy, resulting in slow shutter speeds. It was apparent that both wolf and caribou were well aware of our presence, but the 800mm lens allowed me to remain a comfortable distance without disturbing their struggle.

The wolf circled the caribou for 15 minutes and then backed off and sat down. At this point the bull escaped over a small ridge, out of sight, with the wolf once again following. Although we searched with binoculars, we never saw them again.

As we trudged back down the valley, we were exuberant. Getting wolf behavior such as this is exceedingly difficult in the wild. While many of the photographs that follow were shot in the wild, some have been filmed at a Canadian research compound, specially created to study wolf behavior at close range.

When ultimately the idea came to produce a wolf book, I decided to avoid replicating the multitude of other books on the subject, which were written with a biological slant. Rather, I wanted to create a work that evoked and captured some of the mystery and magic that draws people to them. To this end, writer Greg McNamee has woven a tapestry of wolf lore, and I am struck by the common, recurrent themes voiced by the myriad cultures throughout the Northern Hemisphere; the romantic ideal of the wolf is both a brutal and tender one. To further illustrate the spiritual nature of the wolf and its environment, I have, in five of the photographs in this book, created compositions using the latest in computer technology. All of these illustrations were created digitally, combining my existing photographs. All are identified as "digital illustrations" with a Greek delta sign (▲) in the list of captions on pages 156 and 157. My intent was to re-create scenes I had observed in nature but been unable to capture on film, as in the caribou hunt on page 72 or the white wolf on page 129. Or to create scenes that depict the romanticized wolf of legends and folklore that fill these pages, as in the wolf pack in the snowy woods on page 102.

Even now the place of the wolf in the wilderness is a volatile one. While wolves are being exploited in Alaska to placate hunters, they are being reintroduced into Yellowstone contrary to the wishes of ranchers. A sacrifice for balance is required on our part to ensure the wolf's existence, and that balance must be maintained if the wolf is to survive.

—Art Wolfe
Seattle, Washington

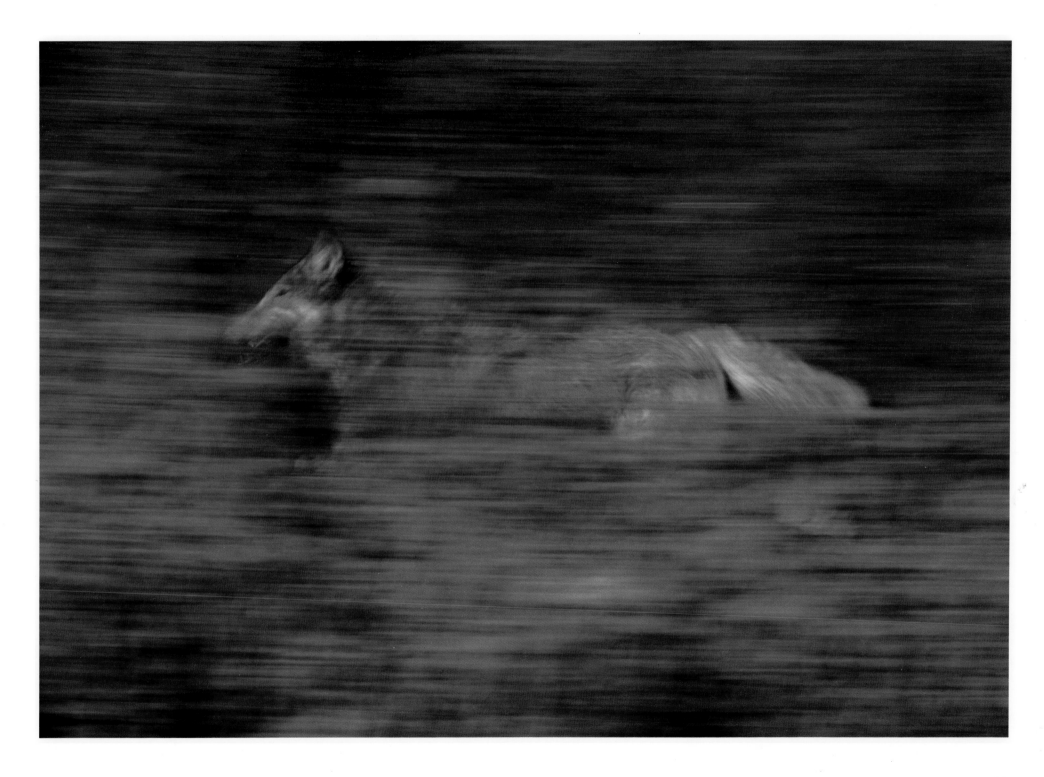

INTRODUCTION

a route of wolves

It begins with a long, chilling note at the upper end of the register, a note that rises improbably higher, breaks, and quavers, hanging in the air, already joined by other voices that shatter the night's stillness in harmony. It throws myriad animals into alarm: rabbits scuttle into their warrens, squirrels take to the higher branches, and deer take flight across the leas. The cry forces humans to confront their special terrors as well. Shepherds draw their greatcoats a little tighter against the darkness. Settlers, fearing impending attack, bar the doors and take up positions at the firing ports. At the full moon, superstitious highlanders search their neighbors for signs of pentagrams. Lara hurls herself, aghast, into Zhivago's sheltering arms in the ice-encased halls of Varykino.

The agent of so much sudden action is the howl of the wolf, the unmistakable nightsong of *Canis lupus*. It has as much power as a tocsin or a call to prayer. In the presence of that ancient ululation we stand face to face with humankind's ancient companions, the "route of wolves," as the 1486 *Book of St. Albans* deems any gathering of lupine others. Too many of us have never heard that music, have never seen such a route in

the flesh. *Canis lupus,* like so many other large predatory species, grows ever rarer in this chewed-up world, quick-marched to the brink of extinction by the drill sergeant of progress.

In the loss of *Canis lupus,* of brother wolf, lies a betrayal of long-forgotten concord, a coexistence that must have begun the moment our gatherer-hunter ancestors saw the mysterious glint of a *tapetum lucidum*—the light-reflecting layer that shields a wolf's eyes and aids its night vision—in the circle of darkness just beyond their campfires. A human called out into the shadows, and a wolf emerged to share in the day's catch, both hunters regarding each other as brethren in a world of catch-as-catch-can.

The claim of kinship between humans and wolves is not in the least far-fetched. In many languages the word for *wolf* carries linguistic markings that place it within the same semantic domain as humans; in others the word fittingly means something like "elder brother" or "elder cousin." Some anthropologists view these ancient attributions as an acknowledgment of the wolf's having once shared a culture of a kind with those gatherer-hunter peoples, self-reliant nomads who themselves are nearly gone today. Both cultures lived as social animals in small bands that encouraged mobility, freestyle hunting, and a certain kind of equality, despite the presence in both bands of alpha male and alpha female, who assumed leadership as the situation required. Both ranged over large areas in the course of the natural year; the wolf once had the largest natural range of any animal species, surpassed only by humans, covering the whole of the continental Northern Hemisphere (and even parts of the Southern, as with the now-extinct Falkland Islands wolf). Both were themselves nearly unaffected by predation from competing species. Both preferred to work the temperate middle altitudes, favoring grassland, broken country, and mild tundra over low deserts or high mountains. Both were commensal, unlike vegetarian species, sharing food not only within their bands but also across species lines.

And both were intelligent killers, rarely wanton, rarely wasteful, who relied on a highly evolved program of signals and language to coordinate their efforts.

Wolf and human, human and wolf. The wolf stands out recognizably in the Paleolithic cave paintings at Lascaux and Altamira, alongside long-extinct aurochs, ibexes, and European bison. Many ancient tribes called themselves after *Canis lupus*—in the eastern Mediterranean alone we find Luvians, Lycians, Lucanians, Dacians, and Hyrcanians, all reflexes of proto–Indo-European terms for *wolf.* It is small wonder that our mythologies are replete with stories of Romulus and Remus; of Artemis and her beloved maiden Kallisto, one of the *Lukeiades korai,* "wolf girls," who honored the goddess; of Chukchee shamans and Mongolian werewolves and Pawnee celestial wolves.

Among Native Americans the wolf took its place among the First People, present at the very beginning of the world. Elizabeth Marshall Thomas attests to the long presence of *Canis lupus* among humans in her fine book *The Hidden Life of Dogs,* recounting the particulars of a den she observed on Baffin Island in the Canadian Arctic. The den had been inhabited by wolves for so long that their paws had worn deep grooves into the slickrock underlying their runway, a runway that skirted the long-established but still far newer settlements of Inuit and Euro-American hunters.

From the time-old gathering of wolves and men came a symbiosis

that has endured to this day. From the wolves who settled among kindly disposed bands of humans came a great polymorphism, an embarrassment of forms: more than 125 breeds of dogs registered with the American Kennel Club descend directly from the ancestral wolf, first domesticated some ten thousand years ago. Going against long-established tradition, the noted biologist Juliet Clutton-Brock argues that *Canis familiaris* should be folded back into *Canis lupus,* at least as a scientific designation, arguing that zoological nomenclature should not be used in the case of domestic animals; a wolf dressed down in dog's clothing is a wolf nonetheless. The fact that wolves and dogs (and, rarely, coyotes) interbreed more or less freely lends support to the notion that all lupine canids ought to be recognized under the single rubric *wolf,* as variations on a single theme.

Physically the largest member of the Canidae—the family that includes dingoes, jackals, hyenas, coyotes, foxes, dholes, fennecs, and wild dogs—the wolf is distinguished by its large, lanky frame; by its long legs and big feet, which lend to its tracks being easily confused with those of the mountain lion; and by its fine, even soft features, notably its almond-colored, wide-shaped eyes. You will rarely see a wolf cringe. It lopes along, sometimes even sauntering, carrying itself with a certain nobility that does not admit of the floppy ears and curly tails of dogs—badges of shame, one might say, that mark its domesticated kin.

Those characteristics seem to be near constants over the 65 million years *Canis lupus* has been evolving, a period that matches the geological evolution of the Nile River. (As the great American conservationist Aldo Leopold rightly remarked, "Only a mountain has lived long enough to listen objectively to the howl of a wolf.") *Canis etruscus,* the Etruscan wolf, from which *Canis lupus* descended directly a million years ago, is

recognizably a wolf, more readily than some hominid fossils show themselves to be on the march to being human. Half a million years ago, during a period of hemispheric glaciation, geographically isolated cousins of the now-extinct *Canis dirus,* the dire wolf, began to mutate into coyotes; although younger than their lupine progenitors, *Canis latrans* somehow, as the biologist R. M. Nowak notes, "represents the ancestral, less specialized condition." That relative lack of specialization has allowed the coyote successfully to colonize areas that the wolf either could not settle or that it has been driven away from; coyotes are now to be found in all fifty states, whereas the wolf, sadly, is all but extinct in the lower forty-eight.

The intelligence of wolves is another long-evolved trait, one that has led to their being valued for so long by discerning humans. They orient themselves three-dimensionally, reconstructing cognitive maps of whole landscapes, an adaptive behavior that must have arisen of necessity as they navigated their way through tangled undergrowth and fallen snags; none of their prey enjoys this clearly advantageous skill. *Canis lupus* can hear over very long distances—on open tundra and in calm weather, as far as ten miles—and at a great range of frequencies, enabling it to track the movements of prey and other predators with the assuredness of a DEW line.

Their intelligence shines through in the way they play: young wolves gambol about happily, play-fighting and pretending to stalk prey, simulations that teach them essential motor and cognitive skills, training for the real world. The interactions of adults and cubs alike are full of meaning: the merest facial gesture, flick of the ear, or slight lift of the tail is enough to send a message that will resound through the pack, the one

wolf sending signals, the others responding with clues that they understand.

Wolves know the conventions of their society, and in the main they play by the rules they have set. (Those who do not become outcasts, the origin of the expression "lone wolf.") Pack wolves are monogamous and unusually attentive to their cubs; if they must leave them for whatever reason, a junior adult will tend to the cubs just as attentively, indicating a well-developed regard for social responsibility. In their twelve years or so of life, wolves will look out for fellow members of their band, seeing to it that none goes hungry.

And they will enjoy one another's company. (In his famous study *The Wolves of Mount McKinley,* the naturalist Adolph Murie remarked, "The strongest impression remaining with me after watching . . . wolves on numerous occasions was their friendliness.") That pleasure is expressed by the very howl that sends other creatures into headlong panic. The alpha male lifts his head and begins a song. Other wolves will chime in with as many as twelve harmonizing tones, a virtual Gregorian chant of the wild. The song will be over in a minute or so, enough time for *Canis lupus* to have declared to the surrounding world something like this: "Listen: we're wolves. This is our pack. Hear our voices: in them we proclaim our existence."

We humans were willing to acknowledge and share that existence for many millennia. It took the transition from gatherer-hunter to pastoral/ agricultural societies in the Neolithic to transform *Canis lupus* into our enemy. The rise of animal domestication and the herding of livestock such as sheep and cattle—easy enough targets for a wolf pack—brought the whole of the wilderness under suspicion. Bears, mountain lions, jaguars, tigers, panthers—any species that competed with *Homo sapiens* for its daily bread—became outlaws, subject to summary execution in the service of a newly urbanized society. Some traces of the old admiration remained, to be sure; throughout Greek literature, for instance, we see a grudging respect particularly for wolves, who "formed bridges with their bodies and crossed the Nile one after another," as Aelian wrote, and both Aristotle and Timotheos of Gaza approvingly noted that when two wolves participated in a kill they shared it in exactly equal parts. Still, they had come to believe that the wolf was a ravenous creature, a symbol of rapine and treacherous cunning; Aeschylus has Orestes proclaim in the *Libation Bearers* that "like a wild-minded wolf, our nature, which we inherit from our mother, cannot be appeased," and an Athenian sent into exile bore the epithet *lykaimiais,* "wolf-thicket man." That equation remained in English stories of the "green man" and the "corn wolf," exiles who returned to a state of nature and who were thenceforward unfit to live in settled society.

Things would grow far worse. In the Middle Ages, that time of fundamentalist frenzy, wolves were captured, tried as witches, drawn and quartered, and hanged in consecrated places like the Louvre—the "wolf field"—while equally innocent humans were killed on the grounds that they were werewolves, witches, and heretics—or, worse, because they did not profess to be Christian. Country by country, *Canis lupus* was extirpated from its former domains across Europe, until by the eighteenth century not a single individual could be found north of the Alps and south of the Baltic Sea, from the Vistula River to Galway Bay. Even in early modern times, abandoned children like the so-called Wild Boy of Aveyron were suspected of being, if not werewolves, then at least the product of an infancy spent in hidden wolf dens in a newly cleansed Europe. The Wild Boy's ward, Father Pierre-Joseph Bonnaterre, thought as much, as he wrote to his bishop: "When he is sitting down, and even when he is eating, he makes a guttural sound, a low murmur; and he rocks his body from right to left or backwards and forwards, with his head and chin up, his mouth closed, and his eyes staring at nothing." This supposedly lupine behavior we would today call autism.

The war on *Canis lupus* came with Europe to the New World, which a Plymouth pilgrim declared to be "a howling wilderness of wolves and savages," a demonic landscape that demanded to be subdued. Within the space of a century the wolf had been nearly eliminated from the Atlantic seaboard, save for a few hardy individuals that took to the swamps or the high country, away from settlement; as European America marched westward, wild America retreated. When cattle began to arrive in the West in large numbers in the 1880s, the war took on a new ferocity: the ranchers were then, as today, determined to make the country their own, and they were not given to sharing it with creatures they perceived to be harmful to their interests. Badgers dig holes in the ground that can snap a wandering cow's leg, hares browse the grasses on which steers fatten, river otters build warrens along streambanks that hinder a calf from reaching water: the ready solution was to wipe out the offending animal.

In this respect *Canis lupus* had two counts against it. It was a predator, of course, given to occasional raids on livestock; never mind that it usually weeded out sick or elderly individuals, a sort of natural eugenics that the naturalist John Bruckner approvingly observed in 1768 in his *Philosophical Survey of the Animal Creation:* "The effects of the carnivo-

rous race are exactly the same as that of the pruning hook, with respect to shrubs which are too luxuriant in their growth, or of the hoe to plants that grow too close together. By the diminution of their number, the others grow to perfection." *Canis lupus* also inhabited just the places where the cattlemen wanted to locate their herds, the grassy, well-watered midlands. Notions of eminent domain could not be reconciled with the presence of wolves.

No sooner was industrial ranching introduced to the West than producers began writing back east to Washington with demands that the federal government use its might to vanquish wolves—not even saving a few for the reservation, as it had for other indigenes. The government succeeded. By 1950 the Mexican gray wolf had been extirpated from the Southwest, the Rocky Mountain gray wolf driven from the central cordillera into Canada, the timber wolf uprooted from the Northwest.

Times change, however. Full as our folklore and popular culture are with images of the Three Little Pigs, Little Red Riding Hood, the Wolf Man, and even a lupine Jack Nicholson, we are coming to appreciate anew the value of both wilderness—the roadless, unsettled areas that are everywhere besieged on our people-crowded planet—and the wild animals who dwell within it. They form a geography of hope, a means of coming to terms with our true inner nature, for finding not the ever-popular "warrior" or Iron John within us but a glimpse, however brief, of our gatherer-hunter, nomadic soul.

Cormac McCarthy writes in his novel *The Crossing* that the wolf is "a being of great order . . . who knows what men do not: that there is no order in the world save that which death has put there." Death has too long been meted out to the wolf, death for a creature who does not share

in our original sin. The wheel is now turning toward the restoration of *Canis lupus* to at least something of its former range, a restoration that will necessarily involve a vigorous program of captive breeding and an equally vigorous campaign to protect individuals still living in the wild. There are not many of them, as the North American statistics tell: Minnesota has a population of perhaps twelve hundred; Alaska—whose governor, Walter Hickel, recently proclaimed, "You can't just let nature run wild"—now only some seven thousand; Wisconsin perhaps twenty; northwestern Montana, perhaps as few as fifteen; and in the whole of Canada, where the wolf has been relatively unmolested, still only some fifty thousand. In the Southwest, no Mexican gray wolves are known to live outside captivity, and from 1991 to 1994 the biologist Julio Guerrero was unable to locate a single wolf in the whole of Mexico's towering Sierra Madre. The figures from other areas tell the same story: along the five-hundred-mile length of the Apennine Mountains of Italy, only a hundred wolves are now thought to exist, most of them in the confines of the Parco Nazionale della Calabria. A like number inhabit a series of preserves in Israel, representing what was once a huge population of Middle Eastern wolves.

It is not enough simply to reintroduce animals like the wolf—or the grizzly, the snow leopard, the cheetah, the tiger, the elephant, to name just a few of the large-animal species that are fading from the earth before our very eyes—to the wild. We need more wilderness, larger untouched areas where nature can indeed run wild without constant human intervention. Animal species need ample room if their gene pools are to remain open-ended and therefore healthy; they need large territories that allow for isolation, the sine qua non for speciation. (The distinguished biologist E. O. Wilson has noted that the number of species doubles with every tenfold increase in untrammeled area.) Wolves in particular require lots of room to roam; a single pack can range over an area as large as sixteen hundred square miles. National parks such as southern Italy's Abruzzo, highland Spain's Coto Doñana, Poland's Bialowiecza, northern Japan's Akau, and Wyoming and Montana's Yellowstone, where wolves enjoy at least some protection, represent an admirable start, but they are not enough. Recent proposals to return such places as New York's Adirondack Mountains, western Montana's Yaak Valley, and southwestern New Mexico's Animas Range to wild status are much surer steps toward bringing North America, at the very least, to some semblance of ecological balance.

Most important, perhaps, restoration will involve a reorientation of our attitudes, closing the circle so that the wolf becomes once more not our enemy but our companion. The texts that follow—folkloric retellings, reports from the field, biological data, and oddments—course over the range of this evolution of thinking about *Canis lupus.* As a species, we have come down a path that has led us from considering the wolf as a witness to Creation and a guide through the world to believing that behind every *tapetum lucidum* lies the soul of the devil. Our understanding has grown to the point that we can now begin to see through the twilight the faint trace of our path home.

When human beings renounced the wolf years ago, we renounced something of our own nature. Through the images and words that follow, we hope to contribute, however modestly, to finding that part of *Homo sapiens* that cannot coexist without *Canis lupus,* that part of us which calls out to the darkness just outside our fires, searching for friends.

—GREGORY MCNAMEE
TUCSON, ARIZONA

26

Wolf's Bride

A man and woman lived with their only child, a daughter, by the sea. They did not know that other people lived in the world. One morning the daughter awoke and went outside. She found a slain caribou. She and her parents cut it up and feasted on it.

That night she awoke to see a wolf's tail in the air. But then it disappeared.

The next night she saw the same thing. The following day she ate seal meat, and then she saw a wolverine's tail.

The next evening she heard footsteps. A young man entered the hut. His clothes were made of wolf fur. Then another man came in, dressed in wolverine fur. He said to the first young man, "I am going to marry her." The two began to argue, and the daughter told them to go outside. They fought for a long time. Then they went away.

When the daughter went outside the next morning, she saw the tracks of a wolf and a wolverine, covered with blood. They disappeared into the forest. She followed them and found a dead wolverine lying in the snow. The wolf tracks continued on.

She went back to her hut, where she found an older man dressed in wolf fur. He said, "Please come with me. My son is badly hurt." They went to the older man's lodge. When they came in, the young man healed upon seeing her. She became his bride.

They came back to her hut and lived with her parents until, after some years, they died. Then they went to the young man's hut and lived with his parents until they also died. The young man distributed two sleds of caribou meat to all the people in the area and announced that he and his wife were going away to a place where sorrow and hardship were not allowed to come. The young man and his wife turned into wolves and left.

CAPE PRINCE OF WALES ESKIMO FOLKTALE

War Helper

When I went on war parties I always took a wolf-hide, bow and arrows, and enemy clothing. When I wanted to go I'd tell two or three friends who might want to go with me—the smaller the group the better, for a little number is harder to detect. I also told my father, but I never told my mother because she would worry. For this reason I never had moccasins made especially for a trip, as many others did; instead, I always kept some on hand. We would start early in the morning. Usually the other men would be waiting outside my tipi. They knew that I stopped for nothing and would go on alone. As soon as I came out we would start, for I didn't want my mother to worry. This time I planned that we would attack the Crows.

After we had walked three or four days we stopped at dawn by a creek for the men to make tobacco offerings to the wolves. Some vowed they would feed all the Wolf Dreamers, if they returned. While they did this, I took my wolf-skin to a nearby hill and, facing the Four Winds, called and cried to the wolves, asking them the whereabouts of the enemy.

When I returned from the hill, we smoked and then I told the men what I had learned—how many days away the enemy was, how large their camp was, whether we would meet an enemy war party and how many men were in it.

GHOST HEAD, SIOUX WARRIOR, CA. 1880

Wolf God Saves a Warrior from Death

Ayoung warrior went into battle against Big Demon, who was terrorizing the countryside. They fought for years. The warrior's sword broke, and he fell into unconsciousness. When he awoke he was standing high in a tree at the foot of the volcano where the Shikot River rises.

He looked down and saw a young boy's corpse lying below him. The god of the mouth of the Shikot River appeared and accused the warrior of cowardice for having fought only one battle. The young warrior retreated and followed the course of the Shishirmuka River toward his home.

He went upstream until he came to a fork in the river. There was a bridge of mist rising high into the sky. He climbed this bridge to the highest heaven, where a doglike creature appeared before him. It had huge fangs and snapped at him until he turned and fled. He ran past the god of the mouth of the Shishirmuka River, the god of the mouth of the Muka River, the god of the mouth of the Iput River, and the god of the mouth of the Shikot River. They all laughed at him while the dog pursued him.

When he arrived at the foot of the volcano where the Shikot River rises, he threw himself on the young boy's corpse. Then he lost consciousness.

He awoke to see a startlingly beautiful young woman. She sang a healing song and blew breath on his body. His wounds instantly healed. The young woman told him, "I am the sister of the Wolf God of the Upper Heavens. Both you and Big Demon died in battle, and you were traveling to the land of the gods. My brother asked me to chase you back and restore you. He also asked me to go to your home and cook your meals for you. I changed into a wolf and did as he asked, restoring you to life."

The warrior returned to his village, and the young woman trailed along after him.

AINU LEGEND

My Blood Is the Blood of a Wolf

There are wolves in the Tigré country. And sometimes a wolf kills a goat, or when they are many, they kill a cow. And men make them give up what they kill; but they do not throw a weapon or a stick or a stone at them, but they throw only pebbles. If the wolves do not heed them, but refuse to give up what they have killed and eat it, men do not wound them with iron or wood or stones for this reason: when the wolf is wounded he sheds blood, and then he dips his tail in the blood and flicks it at him who wounded him. And that man dies if the blood touches him. For this reason they do not throw at the wolves anything but pebbles, because they are afraid of their blood. And so far nobody has ever killed a wolf. And the wolves do not kill men either, but they threaten to kill them. The wolves live in packs, or sometimes they go singly. They are of all colors, and their height is like that of a dog. Men say as a proverb, "My blood is the blood of a wolf," that is to say, it kills him who sheds it.

MENSA BET-ABREHE STORY

Wolf Nature

The wolf, now an endangered species, has become a symbol of all that is right and in harmony with nature. It is modern man who in his ignorance has been wrong and out of step with nature. Not the wolf.

MICHAEL W. FOX, *THE WOLF* (1989)

One Fate

That which happens to men also happens to animals; and one thing happens to them both: as one dies so dies the other, for they share the same breath; and man has no preeminence above an animal: for all is vanity.

All go to one place; all are made of dust, and all return to dust again.

Who knows for certain that the spirit of man goes upward to the heavens and the spirit of the animal descends downward into the earth?

Therefore I perceive that there is nothing better than that a man should rejoice in his own works, for that is his share in life—for who shall bring him to see what shall be after him?

ECCLESIASTES 3: 19–22

A Little Night Music

After I was warmed through and had eaten my supper, I stepped outside once more. The river was still aglisten, and the far shore looked black and somber. An owl hooted back in the spruce, and I knew what that meant in the moonlit glades. A tree cracked sharply with the frost, and then it was still, so still that I could hear the beating of my heart. At last I heard what I was listening for—the long-drawn quavering howl from over the hills, a sound as wild and indigenous to the north as the muskegs or the northern lights. That was wilderness music, something as free and untamed as there is on this earth.

SIGURD F. OLSON, *THE SINGING WILDERNESS* (1956)

Wolf Trees

In his book *On Animals,* Antipater says that wolves bear their young at the time of year when trees that bear nuts or acorns lose their flowers. When they eat these, the wolves' wombs open up. If there is no store of these flowers, however, the offspring die immediately without ever having seen the light of day. In fact, those parts of the world that are not rich in nut trees or oaks are never troubled by wolves.

PLUTARCH, *NATURAL HISTORY* (FIRST CENTURY A.D.)

Wolf Star

The gods gathered one day to make the world so that the people could have someplace to live. They forgot to invite Wolf Spirit. He became angry and put the blame on Paruksti, Western Storm, who carried the people in his whirlwind bag. Whenever he rested the people would emerge and hunt buffalo.

Wolf Spirit sent down Wolf, who came along while Paruksti was asleep and stole the whirlwind bag. Then the people hunted some more, and Wolf shared the meat with them. Paruksti appeared and said, "People, that is Wolf!" They killed Wolf instead of just driving him away, which displeased the gods. They ordered the people to call themselves Skidi, Wolf-People, forevermore, and to keep Wolf Spirit holy. The gods also said that by bringing death to the world, the people also brought death to themselves. The people who killed Wolf became wolves themselves.

Wolf rose into the heavens and became Tskirixki-tiuhats, Star of Deceiver Wolf. He rises before the morning star. The wolves, thinking he is the morning star, howl to greet him.

PAWNEE FOLKTALE

39

Wolf Teaches Magic

Once upon a time a man found a wolf den and decided to dig and get the cubs. The worried mother Wolf came barking and said to him, "Pity my children." But the man took no heed. The mother quickly ran to get the father of the cubs, who came at once to confront the man. But the man ignored the Wolf father also and continued to dig the cubs out from the den. Frustrated, the father Wolf sang a beautiful song: "O man, pity my children and I will teach you one of my magical skills." He ended his plea with a penetrating howl that caused a thick fog to cover the land. Then the Wolf howled again and the fog quickly disappeared.

Awed by the Wolf's gift, the man reconsidered and did not steal the cubs. He thought to himself, "These animals have mysterious gifts." So he tore up his red blanket into small pieces and made pretty Indian red cloth necklaces for the cubs and took the cubs back to their parents.

The father was so thankful that he made this promise to the man: "When you go into battle hereafter, I will accompany you, and bring to pass whatever you wish." Then they soon parted as friends.

In the course of time, the man went to battle against his enemies. As he came into sight of the enemy village, a large Wolf met him saying, "By and by I will sing and you shall take their horses when they least expect it." So the man and the Wolf stopped on a hill close to the enemy village. Fulfilling his promise, the Wolf sang his song. After this he howled, making a high wind arise. The horses fled to the forest, many stopping on the hillside. When the Wolf howled again, the wind died away and a mist arose. So the man, under the cover of the mist, took as many horses as he wished.

DAKOTA SIOUX FOLKTALE

The Gray Wolf and the Orphan

There was an orphan boy who went hunting by himself in the woods. He was a very poor boy and had no friends; so that was why he went off hunting by himself. He went a long way, and did not find anything to kill. At last he saw a very small gray wolf cub. "You are an orphan, too," he said to it. "If you had a mother she would crack your fleas. I will take you for my brother." He went on; he killed a bird and gave it to the weak little wolf. By and by they went to bed on the leaves. In the morning he killed more birds, but the little wolf could not get enough. So they went on many days, but the little wolf did not get fat. In a year's time he did not get fat, but he got tall; he could hunt. The boy was lonesome; he did not like to have no friend but a wolf. One day the wolf brought a baby to him. It was a girl. It was pretty. It had good clothes and beads. The wolf talked, it was the first time. The wolf said: "Go to the village, it is near." He took the baby to the village. It was the chief's baby. He had a grown daughter. The poor boy married her and had plenty of all things. The wolf came one night. He said: "I was fooling. I was not a cub, I was a grandfather. I pitied you and wanted to make your fortune." The wolf went away. The orphan boy cried, but the wolf had made his fortune.

MUSQUAKIE (FOX) FOLKTALE

The Back Woods

Once, when we were travelling on foot not far from the southern boundary of Kentucky, we fell in with a Black Wolf, following a man with a rifle on his shoulders. On speaking with him about this animal, he assured us that it was as tame and as gentle as any dog, and that he had never met with a dog that could trail a deer better. We were so much struck with this account and the noble appearance of the wolf, that we offered him one hundred dollars for it; but the owner would not part with it at any price.

JOHN JAMES AUDUBON,
THE QUADRUPEDS OF NORTH AMERICA (1851)

Signs

Those people at whom a wolf barks will live for a long time. A howling wolf brings a change in the weather.

DELAWARE PROVERBS

Returning to New England

We looked out the window to see a timber wolf sitting on the sloping lawn where our trail descended from the woods. Scruffy, peaceful, observant, she turned her gaze slowly to take in the gardens, the woodpile, jalopy and bikes, the lean-to woodshed, the white clapboard house—the complex scent of human lives. How we kept the dog quiet, I don't know. We knew that wolves did not live in Connecticut. Yet here was a wolf sitting in our yard—a fact that no one's doubting would take away from us. When my father came home from work, he didn't believe us. It must have been a German shepherd or a husky. And it is true that the animal's body bore some resemblance to such pets. But that creature's wary calmness was a thing cultivated in the wild. She had come down from Roundtop, from woods to the west and the north—the patchy wilderness that snaked between houses, suburbs, turnpikes, and cities, obliquely connecting our woods with the Catskills, the Berkshires, the Adirondacks, and the great woods of the Canadian north. Winds blew down from there in winter—once bringing snow so deep we shoveled a tunnel, not a path, leading from our front door. The she-wolf sat for a long time, if the time an experience takes can be measured by its impact. Time, always running too fast or too slow, mercifully left us—until the wolf stood up, turned around, and walked silently back into the mystery of those woods.

ALISON HAWTHORNE DEMING,
TEMPORARY HOMELANDS (1994)

Wolf and Lion (1)

An old lady had a very fine flock of sheep. She cared for them so well that they became famous for their fatness. In time a wolf heard of them and determined to eat them. Night after night he stole up to the old woman's cottage and killed a sheep. The poor woman tried her best to save her animals from harm, but failed.

At last there was only one sheep left of all the flock. Their owner was very sad. She feared that it, too, would be taken away from her, in spite of all she could do. While she was grieving over the thought of this, a lion came to her village. Seeing her sad face, he asked the reason for it. She soon told him all about it. He thereupon offered to do his best to punish the wolf. He himself went to the place where the sheep was generally kept, while the sheep was removed to another place.

In the meantime the wolf was on his way to the cottage. As he came, he met a fox. The fox was somewhat afraid of him and prepared to run away. The wolf, however, told him where he was going, and invited him to go too. The fox agreed, and the two set off together. They arrived at the cottage and went straight to the place where the sheep generally slept. The wolf at once rushed upon the animal, while Fox waited a little behind. Just as Fox was deciding to enter and help Wolf, there came a bright flash of lightning. By the light of it, the fox could see that the wolf was attacking not a sheep but a lion. He ran away hastily, shouting as he went, "Look at his face! Look at his face!"

During the flash, Wolf did look at the pretended sheep. To his dismay he found he had made a great mistake. At once he began to make humble apologies, but in vain. Lion refused to listen to any of his explanations, and speedily put him to death.

ASHANTI LEGEND

The Wolf and the Sheep

In long past times there lived a householder in a certain hill-village. His shepherd went afield to tend his flocks. As the shepherd returned to the village at sunset from tending them, an old ewe which lagged somewhat behind was seized by a wolf.

"Aunt, aunt," said the wolf, "is it well with you? Aunt, aunt, do you seem to find yourself comfortable all alone in the forest?"

Moreover the wolf said, "Do you think, O sheep, whom I have addressed by the name of aunt, that you will escape after having pinched my tail, and also plucked hairs out of my tail?"

The sheep replied, "How could I have pinched your tail, seeing that it is behind you, and I have been going in front of you?"

But the wolf said, "Which way then did you come, seeing that my tail spreads all over the four parts of the world, together with the ocean and the hill-villages?"

The sheep rejoined, "As I had heard beforehand from my kinsmen that your tail, O best one, spreads everywhere, I came through the air."

The wolf replied, "O mother, if you came through the air, you must have scared away the herd of gazelles which I meant to feed upon."

Having thus spoken, the malefactor made a spring, tore off the sheep's head, and having killed the sheep, devoured its flesh.

NEPALI FOLKTALE

Wolf and Mouse

A wolf and a mouse once planted onions together on a piece of land they rented. The onions grew large—blessings be on the Prophet—and the wolf said, "Brother mouse, let's harvest them."

The wolf said, "Whatever is above the ground is mine. Whatever is below the ground is yours." He knew nothing of agriculture, and thought the large leaves were the best part. He gathered his relatives, and together they harvested the leaves and took them to his threshing-floor. In two or three days the leaves had withered to dust. The mouse and his relatives, on the other hand, sold their onions for more than three hundred pounds.

The next year the wolf said, "Brother mouse, let's plant wheat."

He continued, "This time I will take the root."

When harvest came, the mouse took the grain, while the wolf took the stems and roots. The mouse had enough wheat to earn two hundred pounds, while the wolf had nothing of value. So the wolf went to the mouse's threshing-floor and demanded the grain.

The mouse said, "Let's race to the top of the grain. Whoever gets there first gets it." The wolf ran faster than the mouse, who hid and told the wolf he was atop the grain pile. The wolf gave up the chase, saying, "I will leave these things in the hands of Allah."

MODERN EGYPTIAN FOLKTALE

Wolf Teaches the People How to Hunt

When the people were wandering after the emergence, they came to Black-god's house, *adaahwiidzo*. Black-god and Talking-god brought them inside and showed them an abundance of mountain sheep at the east door, an abundance of corn and squash and other plants at the south door. At the north door came bad things like snow and storms. Fawn was their protector. Fawn said, "If you shoot me and I cry out, then bad things will befall you unless you know how to pray. Then you can move in peace."

Wolf showed the people how to pray. He told them to howl four times to the north. Wolf also gave them his voice, telling them to use it when they hunted. He said that if they did not use it they would be surrounded by deer but could never hit them. Fawn said, "Yes, we will put an empty deerskin out there, and all your arrows will fall on it."

Talking-god added, "Lion, Bobcat, Tiger, Wildcat, and Wolf are those who, like the people, hunt from their homes. They tiptoe while hunting. You must use the word 'tiptoe' when you hunt—but never speak it inside your house." The people obeyed, and ever since then the people have had more deer than they could ever eat.

NAVAJO DEER HUNTINGWAY LEGEND

A Land Subdued

When I consider that the nobler animals have been exterminated here—the cougar, panther, lynx, wolverine, wolf, bear, moose, deer, beaver, turkey, etc.—I cannot but feel as if I lived in a tamed, and, as it were, emasculated country. . . . I should not like to think that some demigod had come before me and picked out some of the best of the stars. I wish to know an entire heaven and an entire earth.

HENRY DAVID THOREAU, *JOURNALS* (1856)

Vade Mecum

Do not divert your love from tangible things. Continue to love what is good, simple, and ordinary: animals and flowers. Keep the balance true.

RAINER MARIA RILKE (CA. 1915)

Chains of Life

There are no compacts among lions and men, and wolves and lambs have no concord.

THE ILIAD XXII, 262

Wolf Saviors

It is said that Mount Parnassus and its valley were named after the hero Parnassus, who found them by bird divination. He founded the city of Parnassus, which was inundated during Deukalion's flood. Its inhabitants were saved by following the howls of wolves onto the heights of Mount Parnassus, and when they rebuilt their town they named it Leukoreia, "City of Wolves."

PAUSANIAS X.6.2

Wolf's Ghost

In a village in the Western desert there lived a herdsman named Ts'ang. His wife noticed that of late he had not been eating when he returned to their *ger,* and she asked him where he had had his meal.

He replied, "My wife, it is this way. I kept on passing the temple at the oasis where that wolf's skin hangs in honor of the gods, and I could not resist jumping into it. When I do so I become a wolf. The next time I turn into a wolf, however, I fear that I will eat you. Please do this. Tomorrow bar the door. Leave a straw figure filled with pig's intestines by the door outside. Do this and I will spare you."

The next day the wolf came to the *ger* and tried to break down the door. When he failed he had at the straw figure.

Ts'ang's fellow villagers came with clubs and hatchets and chased him away. Someone cut off a piece of his tail.

Ts'ang never returned. Every now and then a herdsman will report that he has seen a bobtailed wolf against the hills, howling sadly to himself, voicing his sorrow.

CHINESE FOLKTALE

Wolf as Mirror

Humankind needs the wolf. We see in the wolf those values and traits without which we as a species will perish. A human being without a family, without roots, without work, a human being without a sense of place, of location, of community, is like a wolf without its pack, its home territory, its sense of belonging and purpose and security. The person becomes alienated, fearful, opportunistic, amoral, and, above all, alone. A society—or worse, a world—built of such people has lost its center, its heritage, and quite possibly determined its downfall. The wolf . . . reminds us of what we cannot forget: that our origins are out there, in the cold, windy outback of time, and that we are, despite all of the tinsel and trappings of civilization, still very much a part of that wild nature.

John A. Murray, *Wildlife in Peril* (1987)

Wolf and Mountain Lion Go Hunting

One time Wolf and Mountain Lion were camped together. They were both very great deer hunters, but they did not know which one was the best hunter. This way they decided to see who was the most successful hunter. They both started out when it got dark in the evening, each going in a different direction. Wolf hunted all night long, and finally killed one deer. He brought it back to camp. Pretty soon Mountain Lion came in with a deer also. Mountain Lion had hunted almost all night, too, and traveled a great way, as had Wolf. Mountain Lion said to Wolf, "You wear your claws off when you hunt because you run so much." Then Wolf said to Mountain Lion, "You wear all the fur off your elbows and legs the way you hunt, because you crawl along so much."

WHITE MOUNTAIN APACHE LEGEND

The Hunter Hunted

One may well ask, doesn't it almost border on the absurd to waste words on the death of an animal in a world in which millions are suffering from hunger, a world with an ever-increasing population, escalating use of energy, and a hyper-exponential increase in destruction of the environment, while all the time the rich grow richer and the poor grow poorer? Certainly—but for the fact that the extinction of an animal species is symptomatic of the threat to ourselves. Once upon a time the wolf was a symbol of our fear of nature, our struggle against it: now it has become a symbol of our fear for nature, the environment that is all of ours. In the light of the consequences that are now becoming evident, the worst possible advice that could have been given to humanity was: Make yourselves masters of the world. It is becoming clear to us that it should have been: Adapt yourselves to life in the world. Even though it sometimes takes generations for new ideas to be accepted, there is some hope for us all—as well as for that hunted hunter the wolf.

ERIC ZIMEN, THE WOLF (1978)

72

The Wolf and the Seven Kids

Once upon a time there was a she-goat who had seven kids. One day she went into the forest to fetch some food. She called all seven and said, "Dears, I'm going into the forest. Be on your guard against the wolf. If he gets in here, he'll devour you. He is a rascal and often uses disguises, but you can tell him right away by his growly voice and black paws."

"Dear mother," the kids replied, "we'll be careful. Don't worry about us."

The she-goat left, relieved. Soon someone was at the door, saying, "Open the door, dears, I'm back with food for all of us." The kids knew it was the wolf by his growly voice.

"No," they said. "You're not our mother. She has a gentle voice, but yours is growly. Go away, wolf!"

The wolf went to a shop and bought a piece of chalk. He ate it, and it softened his voice. He went back, knocked at the door, and said, "Open the door, dears, I'm back with food for all of us." The wolf had his black paw on the stoop, and when the kids saw it they said, "No. Our mother has white feet. Go away, wolf!"

The wolf went to a bakery and said, "Put some flour on my leg." The baker at first refused, but the wolf threatened to devour him. He then sprinkled flour on the wolf's paw to make it white. The wolf went back, knocked, and said, "Open the door, dears, I'm back with food for all of us."

The kids said, "Let's see your paw." The wolf raised his paw up to the windowsill, and when the kids saw that it was white, they opened the door. The wolf came inside. The kids tried to hide when they saw that it was really him. The first jumped under the kitchen table, the second into the bed, the third into the oven, the fourth into the coal scuttle, the fifth into the cupboard, the sixth beneath the washbasin, and the seventh into the grandfather clock. The wolf found them one by one and ate them up, all but the one who hid inside the clock. Then the wolf, full and drowsy, wandered outside and fell asleep under an elm tree.

Soon the she-goat returned. She was alarmed to see that the furniture was all upended, the washbasin was shattered, the bedclothes were torn from the bed, and her children were all gone. Finally the youngest called out, "Dear mother, I'm inside the clock!" He told her that the wolf had eaten his brothers. The she-goat wept bitter tears.

After a while she went down to the meadow, distraught, with the youngest kid alongside her. They saw the wolf lying sound asleep. She saw something wriggling in his stomach. Thinking that her kids could still be alive, she sent the youngest home to get a pair of scissors and a needle and some thread. Then she cut the wolf's gut open, and one by one the kids jumped out.

The she-goat said, "Go find some big stones. We'll fill this rascal's belly with them."

The kids gathered stones and filled the wolf's stomach with them. The she-goat stitched the wolf up again, while the wolf kept on snoring. When he awoke, he went to the well to get a drink. As he walked, the stones rattled around in his belly. When he arrived at the well he leaned over to pull up a bucket of water, and the stones made him topple over. He drowned while the kids gamboled around the well in celebration.

BOHEMIAN FOLKTALE

Wolf Daughter

Long ago, animals lived in the same way as people do today. One day a wolverine came to a village and asked to marry the daughter of a family of wolves. The wolf-girl's mother frowned on the idea, but she finally gave her permission. The wolverine and the wolf-girl had a number of children, all but one of them wolverines. That one was a wolf.

The wolverine cursed the wolves to bring them bad luck in hunting. He refused to feed them himself, telling them that he had no meat to give to his mother-in-law. But he had plenty of beaver meat stored up.

Finally the wolves succeeded in killing a moose. Then the wolverine came to their camp and asked for moose meat. The mother-in-law said, "Yes. But when you eat moose meat you have to shut your eyes." When he closed his eyes, the mother-in-law killed the wolverine with a club. Then she ordered the wolves to kill all the wolverine children, but to spare the wolf, for it shared their nature.

ROCK CREE FOLKTALE

Tres Hermanas
Wolf

A beautiful maiden who always dressed in white buckskin once went to a spring in the Tres Hermanas Mountains to fetch water. Her people waited and waited for her return, but she did not come back to their camp. They went to the spring and found her *olla*. Then they found her tracks going higher up into the mountains. They followed her as far as they could, but then her tracks went straight up the stone face of the summit and disappeared.

Her people called for the shaman to search out her lost spirit. He sang and smoked for four days, and then said, "She is alive up there in the mountains." He knew the mountains well.

They went to the stone face and sang. The cliff opened onto a hall full of wolves, bears, and mountain lions. The shaman sang some more, and the people and animals joined in. Another door opened, and there stood the maiden with a bear, who changed into a wolf.

"Come with us," the shaman said. But the maiden refused, saying, "Stay close to this holy place; keep your camp near these mountains. I will always be among you, and no enemy will trouble you. Keep sight of this place." The people returned to their camp, but they decided to leave the Tres Hermanas Mountains. Four days later they were massacred.

At night a wolf howls in the Tres Hermanas Mountains, calling for her people to return.

CHIRICAHUA APACHE FOLKTALE

79

Distorted Images

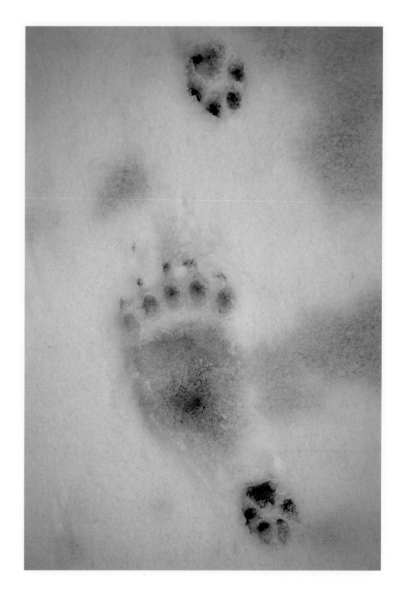

We need another and wiser and perhaps a more mystical concept of animals. Remote from universal nature, and living by complicated artifice, man in civilization surveys the creature through the glass of his knowledge and sees thereby a feather magnified and the whole image in distortion. We patronize them for their incompleteness, for their tragic fate of having taken form so far below ourselves. And therein we err, and greatly err. For the animal shall not be measured by man. In a world older and more complete than ours they move finished and complete, gifted with extensions of the senses we have lost or never attained, living by voices we shall never hear. They are not brethren, they are not underlings; they are other nations, caught with ourselves in the net of life and time, fellow prisoners of the splendor and travail of the earth.

HENRY BESTON, *THE OUTERMOST HOUSE* (1928)

The Outlaw Lover

People become what they are named. Here a Saxon warrior carrying the evocative appellation Wulf has taken to the forests and become an outlaw over the love of a young woman, the speaker here, who has been married to another warrior named Eadwacer. Hunted like the creature for which he is named, Wulf circles the palisades of Eadwacer's island fortress, waiting, watching, biding his time, while his imprisoned lover yearns for the freedom he can bring her. This Anglo-Saxon poem, taken from the ninth-century Exeter Book, accords our wolf an unusual degree of sympathy.

The men of my tribe treat him as game:
if he comes to the camp they will slaughter him.

Our destiny is riven.

Wulf is on one island, and I am on this one.
Mine is a fortress: the swamps encircle it

and it is defended by the
strongest warriors.
If he comes here they will slaughter him.

Our destiny is riven.

It was raining, and I cried by the fire,
thinking of Wulf's long wanderings;
one of our captains took me in his arms.
It gladdened me, but it saddened me too.

Wulf, my Wulf, wanting you
brought me heartsickness, your absence,
this emptiness in my heart;
this is not hunger, as they say.

Do you hear me, Eadwacer? Our wild
Wulf takes to the woods.
What was never fixed is easily destroyed,
like our lives together.

Yellow Eyes

Wolf Woman lived not far from Skeleton Man. One day Wolf Woman went looking for food and passed Skeleton Man's place. Skeleton Man was doing something unusual, and she stopped to look.

Skeleton Man was singing, "Hi ya, hi ya, hey!" Then his eyes flew outside his head south to the horizon. Then they flew back and went into his head again. "I have seen many new things," Skeleton Man told Wolf Woman.

Wolf Woman said, "It is a good song."

"Yes," Skeleton Man replied. "When I sing it I travel. Just now I passed over a canyon that is full of deer and rabbits."

"Will you teach me to sing it?" Wolf Woman asked.

"Yes," Skeleton Man said. "Sing it facing south and do not move."

Wolf Woman sang, "Hi ya, hi ya, hey!" Her eyes left her head. She saw the canyon and all the animals it contained. But her eyes did not return. She had moved.

Finally she realized that she was not facing south. She felt around and found what she thought were her eyes. They did not give her good sight at first.

Wolf Woman went home. Her pups fled when they saw her, for she had large yellow eyes. She had replaced her eyes with yellow gourds. For that reason wolves have yellow eyes. They live everywhere.

HOPI LEGEND

84

Leto and the Wolves

When Leto had given birth to Apollo and Artemis on the island Astoria, she came to Lycia, carrying the children to the bathing places of the river Xanthus. No sooner had she come into that country than she found herself at the spring Melite. There she stopped to bathe the children before she proceeded to the Xanthus. But herdsmen who wanted water for their herds sent her away. Wolves met her and fawned over the goddess and acted as her escort all the way to the river Xanthus. When she had drunk of its water and bathed the children, she consecrated the Xanthus to Apollo, and to the country—which had formerly been called Trimilis—she gave the name of Lycia from the wolves that had led her here. Then she returned to the spring to punish the herdsmen who had driven her away. They were still watering their cattle at the spring; Leto therefore changed them all into frogs. She struck them smartly on their backs and shoulders with a stone, threw them into the spring, and condemned them to a watery existence.

ANTONINUS LIBORALIS (A.D. 150)

Wolf and Lion (2)

Lion roared, saying, "In the world there is not another equal to me in strength; only my friend, Elephant Ngola'Aniinii, and Red-ant of Malemba, whose touch is pain, they are equal to me."

But the Wolf, who had lurked in the thicket, then got up, moved off a short distance, and said, "Lion, you told a lie, saying 'in the world there is not another equal to me.' The Know-much [human] is stronger." He walked a little, and said again, "The Hang-arms [gorilla] is stronger!"

Lion looked at Wolf. Anger took him, and he chased Wolf, but gave him up.

Therefore they hate each other: because Lion once told a lie, but Wolf exposed him.

MBUNDU LEGEND

Escape

It's the she-wolf," Bill whispered.

The dogs had lain down in the snow, and he walked past them to join his partner at the sled. Together they watched the strange animal that had pursued them for days and that had already accomplished the destruction of half their dog-team.

After a searching scrutiny, the animal trotted forward a few steps. This it repeated several times, till it was a short hundred yards away. It paused, head up, close by a clump of spruce trees, and with sight and scent studied the outfit of the watching men. It looked at them in a strangely wistful way, after the manner of a dog; but in its wistfulness there was none of the dog affection. It was a wistfulness bred of hunger, as cruel as its own fangs, as merciless as the frost itself.

It was large for a wolf, its gaunt frame advertising the lines of an animal that was among the largest of its kind.

"Stands pretty close to two feet an' a half at the shoulders," Henry commented. "An' I'll bet it ain't far from five feet long."

"Kind of strange color for a wolf," was Bill's criticism. "I never seen a red wolf before. Looks almost cinnamon to me."

The animal was certainly not cinnamon-colored. Its coat was the true wolf-coat. The dominant color was gray, and yet there was to it a faint

reddish hue—a hue that was baffling, that appeared and disappeared, that was more like an illusion of the vision, now gray, distinctly gray, and again giving hints and glints of a vague redness of color not classifiable in terms of ordinary experience.

"Looks for all the world like a big husky sled-dog," Bill said. "I wouldn't be s'prised to see it wag its tail."

"Hello, you husky!" he called. "Come here, you, whatever your name is."

"Ain't a bit scairt of you," Henry laughed.

Bill waved his hand at it threateningly and shouted loudly; but the animal betrayed no fear. The only change in it that they could notice was an accession of alertness. It still regarded them with the merciless wistfulness of hunger. They were meat, and it was hungry; and it would like to go in and eat them if it dared.

"Look here, Henry," Bill said, unconsciously lowering his voice to a whisper because of what he meditated. "We've got three cartridges. But it's a dead shot. Couldn't miss it. It's got away with three of our dogs, an' we oughter put a stop to it. What d'ye say?"

Henry nodded his consent. Bill cautiously slipped the gun from under the sled-lashing. The gun was on the way to his shoulder, but it never got there. For in that instant the she-wolf leaped sidewise from the trail into the clump of spruce trees and disappeared.

The two men looked at each other. Henry whistled long and comprehendingly. "I might have knowed it," Bill chided himself aloud, as he replaced the gun. "Of course a wolf that knows enough to come in with the dogs at feedin' time, 'd know all about shooting-irons."

JACK LONDON, *WHITE FANG* (1906)

How the Wolf Lost His Tail

One day the wolf and the fox were out together, and they stole a dish of crowdie. Now the wolf was the bigger beast of the two, and he had a long tail like a greyhound, and great teeth. The fox was afraid of him, and did not dare to say a word when the wolf ate most of the crowdie, and left only a little at the bottom of the dish for him, but he determined to punish him for it; so the next night when they were out together the fox said, "I smell a very nice cheese," and pointed to the moonshine on the ice. "There it is."

"And how will you get it?" said the wolf.

"Well, stop you here till I see if the farmer is asleep, and if you keep your tail on it, nobody will see you or know that it is there. Keep it steady. I may be some time coming back."

The wolf lay down and laid his tail on the moonshine in the ice, and kept it for an hour till it was fast. Then the fox, who had been watching him, ran in to the farmer and said: "The wolf is there; he will eat up the children—the wolf! the wolf!"

Then the farmer and his wife came out with sticks to kill the wolf, but the wolf ran off leaving his tail behind him, and that is why the wolf is stumpy-tailed to this day, though the fox has a long brush.

SCOTTISH FOLKTALE

Wolves and Stags

One day all the wolves of the north gathered alongside the Nass River to visit. They sang the usual wolf songs, and they sang so loudly that all the creatures of the forest fled in panic. Some of the fish hid under cobbles or burrowed into the riverbed, while the salmon, trying to escape, jumped this way and that, over waterfalls and rapids, swimming upriver to safety. Even the sun hid itself in the clouds. The moon, though, settled above the treetops to hear the wolves' song.

The wolves eventually grew hoarse, so they told potlatch stories about their brave deeds. They talked this way until dawn.

Across the river a group of stags, hidden in morning fog, began to laugh at them, for animals only appreciate their own language. The sun reappeared and melted away the mist.

"This is how we laugh," said one wolf, baring his sharp fangs. The stags tried to laugh through their tight mouths, showing their stumpy teeth. The wolves, seeing that the stags could not fight them, set out in chase. They chase the stags to this very day.

TSIMSHIAN LEGEND

The Kill, Yellowstone
National Park, Wyoming

Among the canine family, wolves, coyotes, and foxes are opportunistic hunters, eating everything from fruit and mice to birds and snakes. Bringing down larger prey is a matter which usually requires the strength of a pack; however, in the story depicted in this photographic series a single coyote was able to ambush a mule deer, and bring it down alone. The photographer was able to film the entire episode, which lasted about an hour, from the snowy banks of the Yellowstone River.

Yellowstone winters are long and bitterly cold, and this thickly furred coyote was very hungry. Stalking the deer to the banks of the river, the coyote attacked the deer, injuring its nose. The deer fled into the river where the coyote declined to follow, and a standoff began.

Usually a coyote would not hesitate to follow its prey into water; however, this coyote was quite hesitant to do so; daunting was not only the size of the prey, but the icy, churning water as well. Driven by hunger, it simply decided to wait the deer out.

For the deer, escape to the far bank was impossible; it was shocked by the attack, weakened by the initial struggle, and overwhelmed by cold. Facing death either by freezing water or at the jaws of the coyote, the deer finally flung itself out of the river at its assailant.

A battle ensued, with neither combatant willing to give in. When the deer charged, the coyote grabbed the deer's muzzle within its jaws. The deer attempted to run away as the coyote latched onto its hind leg, thwarting escape. Bloodied and exhausted, the deer was taken down at last by the tenacious coyote.

After the coyote killed the deer, other coyotes came to feed as well. Remaining the dominant feeder of the pack, the victor allowed others to have their turns.

Coyote Tricks Wolf Again

One day Coyote went to hunt buffaloes. For five days he searched for them. He was becoming hungry. Then he met Wolf.

"Where are you going?" Wolf asked. "Just traveling around," Coyote said, as he always did. Wolf departed and Coyote kept searching. He soon heard a wagon clattering along, loaded with meat. He could smell that it was buffalo meat, but he was too small to jump into the bed of the wagon and steal some. He circled around a hill in front of the wagon. There he lay down and played dead. The driver of the wagon saw him, halted his team, and inspected Coyote. "I'll skin him later," he decided, and threw him into the wagon. Coyote ate until he nearly burst, then jumped out and set off for home. He soon met Wolf, who was tracking the meat by its smell.

Wolf said, "You're not the same coyote I met before, are you? You look like him, but he was starving, and you're sated." "It's me," said Coyote. He told Wolf about the wagon and the coyote trick he'd played, and encouraged Wolf to follow his example. He did, and the driver stopped as before. This time, determined not to get fooled, he hit Wolf several times with his whip. Nearly dead, Wolf managed to run away.

KIOWA STORY

Coyote Lets Wolf Go Hungry

One day Coyote visited Maítso, Wolf. Wolf took two wooden-headed reed arrows down from the rafters of his hut. He pulled out the points and rubbed them against his thigh, wetted them in his mouth, and buried them in the hot ashes of his hearth. After waiting a while he raked the ashes. Where the points once lay now were two mincemeat puddings. Wolf put them on a grass mat and urged Coyote to eat his fill. Coyote ate, and when he left, he asked Wolf to come to his house for a visit two days later. Wolf went to Coyote's house. Coyote took down two arrowheads, as Wolf had done, rubbed them against his thigh, wetted them in his mouth, and buried them in the hot ashes of his hearth. After waiting a while he raked the ashes. Where the points once lay now were two small pieces of charcoal. Coyote went on talking to Wolf as if nothing had gone awry, until Wolf, sure that he would go hungry if he remained, gave up and left.

NAVAJO LEGEND

The Wolves of the Prairie

Capt Clark found a den of young wolves in the course of his walk today and also saw a great number of those anamals; they are very abundant in this quarter, and are of two species. [The] small woolf or burrowing dog of the praries are the inhabitants almost invariably [of] open plains; they usually ascociate in bands of ten or twelve sometimes more and burrow near some pass or place much frequented by game; not being able alone to take a deer or goat they are rarely ever found alone but hunt in bands; they frequently watch and seize their prey near their burrows; in these burrows they raise their young and to them they also resort when pursued; when a person approaches them they frequently bark, their note being precisely that of the small dog. [They] are of an intermediate size between that of the fox and dog, very active fleet and delicately formed; ears large erect and pointed the head long and pointed more than that of the fox; tale long and bushey; the hair and fur also resembles the fox tho' is much coarser and inferior.

[They] are of a redish brown colour, the eye of a deep sea green colour small and piercing. [Their] tallons are reather longer than those of the ordinary wolf or that common to the atlantic states, none of which are to be found in this quarter, nor I believe above the river Plat. The large woolf found here is not as large as those of the atlantic states. [They] are lower and thicker made shorter leged. [Their] colour, which is not effected by the seasons, is a grey or blackish brown every intermediate shade from that to a creen [cream] coloured white; these wolves resort [to] the woodlands and are also found in the plains, but never take refuge in the ground or burrow so far as I have been able to inform myself. [We] scarcely see a gang of buffalo without observing a parcel of those faithful shepherds on their skirts in readiness to take care of the mamed wounded. [The] large wolf never barks, but howls as those of the atlantic states do.

THE JOURNALS OF LEWIS AND CLARK

Magyar Wolves

A young man, born into the depths of poverty, was ordered to leave his home to discover the wide world, thus freeing his family of the burden of feeding him. In the forest, he lost his way. Half blind with hunger, he fell into a magical well and was brought to full health by its restorative mud. In turn he applied healing mud packs to a wounded mouse, a half-crushed bee, and a maimed wolf, each of whom promised him the aid of its race in time of need.

The young man made his way to the royal capital, where the king ordered him to perform a number of impossible tasks. Calling a phalanx of wolves to his aid, the young man lay siege to the king's fortress, and his allies tore its unfortunate occupants to shreds. The young man married the sole survivor, the king's beautiful daughter, and settled down to a life of wealth, while the wolves and mice and bees returned to the woods from whence they had come. All of them are immortal.

HUNGARIAN FOLKTALE

The Wolves of New England

The Woolves be in some respect different from them in other countries; it was never knowne yet that a Woolfe ever set upon a man or a woman. Neither doe they trouble Horses or Cowes; but Swine, Goate and red Calves, which they take for Deare, be often destroyed by them, so that a red Calfe is cheaper than a blacke one in that regard in some places; in the time of Autumn and in the beginning of the Spring, these ravenous rangers doe most frequent at English habitations, following the Deere which come down at that time to those parts. They be made much like a Mungrell, being big boned, lanky launched, deepe breasted, having a thicke necke, and head, pricke ears, and long snoute with dangerous teeth, long staring haire, and a great bush tails; it is thought of many that our English Mastiffes might be too hard for them; but it is no such matter, for they care no more for an ordinary Mastiffe, than an ordinary Mastiff cares for a Curre; many good dogges have been spoyled by them. Once a faire Greyhound hearing them at their Cowlings run out to chide them, who was torne in peeces before he could be rescued. One of them makes no more bones to runne away with a Pigge, than a Dogge to runne away with a Marrow bone. It is observed that they have no joints from their head to the tails, which prevents them from leaping, or sudden turning, as may appease by what I shall shew you. A certaine man having shot a Woolfe, as he was feeding upon a Swine, breaking his leg onely, he knew not how to devise his death; on a suddaine, the Woolfe being a blacke one, he was loath to spoyle his furre with a second shot, his skin being worth five or six pound Sterling; wherefore hee resolved to get him by the tayle, and thrust him into a river that was hard by; which effected, the Woolfe being not able to turns his joyntless body to bite him, was taken.

That they cannot leape may appears by this Woolfe, whose mouth watering at a few Moore impaled Kiddes, would neede leaps over a five-footed pale to get at them; but his foote slipping in the rise, he fell shorrt of his desire, and being hung in the Carpenters stockes, howled so loud, that he frightened away the Kids, and called the English, who killed him. These be killed daily in some place or other, either by the English, or Indian; who have a certaine rate for every head. Yet there is little hope of their utter destruction, the Countrey being so spacious, and they so numerous, travelling in the Swamps by Kennels: sometimes ten or twelve are of a

company. Late at night, and early in the morning, they set up their Cowlings and call their companies together, at night to hunt, at morning to sleepe. . . .

WILLIAM A. WOOD,

NEW ENGLAND'S PROSPECT (1635)

Wolverine and the Wolves

Wolverine, the devil, who was often killed and just as often returned from the dead, was crossing a frozen meadow in deepest winter. The wind blew like knives, and sleet, frost, and hail combined against him. Wolverine was tough, and he did not mind so much. Still, he was glad to hear the long, mournful howl of a pack of pleasant wolves, and he answered in their language (for Wolverine knows many languages). He was soon surrounded by fifteen or twenty gamboling wolves, who danced, rolled over, barked, and nipped at one another out of sheer joy at having met him.

The sagamore, the elder wolf, said, "Stay with us the night, safe from the ruffians of the woods." Wolverine accepted. He ate dried meat with the wolves and sat by their fire long into the night, all with an insouciance that made the wolves grin widely. The sagamore then asked the younger wolves to cover Wolverine carefully so that he would stay warm in his sleep. But Wolverine shook them off, preferring the cold to their solicitude.

The next morning the sagamore said, "Uncle, you have a hard three days' travel before you, and you will find none of our people to guide you. I give you this charm to keep you safe. Hold it over dried wood and then jump over it. Tell no one else, though. You are the first who is not of our people to know this."

Wolverine went. That night he stopped to make camp. He thought, "They are lying. They mock me." Although he was proud and vain, he decided to try the charm. He built up sticks and jumped over them, and they burst into flame.

"Well," Wolverine thought, "I know the freeze will break tonight, and it will grow so warm that I will burn up with their fire." And so he extinguished it.

That night came an even harder freeze, and Wolverine died, having spurned the wolves' gift. He recovered, though, for he has been seen many times ever since then.

PASSAMAQUODDY FOLKTALE

Wolf Soldiers

Etokah-Wechastah is the god of the south, of warm weather. He is assisted by crows and plovers. Wezeattah-Wechastah is the god of the north, of snowstorms. He has wolves for soldiers. When they meet they do battle. Sometimes Etokah-Wechastah wins, and then the birds beat the wolves to death with their warclubs. More often Wezeattah-Wechastah wins, and then the wolves devour the birds and run freely over the world.

DAKOTA LEGEND

Crow and Wolf

Crow was hungry. So was Wolf. Crow stole some smoked fish from a rack. A boy shot him with an arrow and he died. Then he threw Crow into the ocean.

Crow drifted to shore, rotten. Wolf came along and blew life into him, saying, "Return!"

Crow said, "Hey, I was sleeping." Wolf said, "No, you were dead. You were full of worms." Crow cawed his thanks and flew away.

YUKAGHIR FOLKTALE

A World of Wolves

In Norway there are 3. kinds of wolues, and in Scandinauia the wolues fight with Elkes. It is reported that there are wolues in Italy, who when they looke upon a man, cause him to be silent that hee cannot speake. The French-men call those Wolues which have eaten of the flesh of men Encharnes. Among the Crotoniat in Meotis and divers other parts of the world, wolues do abound: there are some few in France, but none at al in England. . . .

There are divers kinds of wolues in the world. . . . The first which is swift hath a greater head than other wolues, and likewise greater legs fitted to run, white spots on the belly, round members, his colour betwixt red and yellow, he is very bold, howleth fearefully, having firy-flaming eies, and continually wagging his head. The second kind hath a greater and larger body then this, being swifter then all other; betimes in the morning he being hungry, goeth abroad to hunt his prey, the sides and tails are of a silver colour, he inhabiteth the Mountaines, except in the winter time, wherein he descendeth to the Gates of Citties or Townes, and boldly without feare killeth both Goates and sheepe, yet by stealth and secretly.

The third kind inhabiteth . . . sharp and inaccessible places, being worthily for beauty preferred before the others, because of his Golden resplendent haires: and therefore my Author saith . . . that he is not a wolfe but some wilde Beast excelling a Wolfe. He is exceeding strong, especially being able with his mouth and teeth to bite asunder not only stones, but Brasse and Iron: He feareth the Dog star and heate of summer, reiocying more in cold then in warme weather, therefore in the Dog daies he hideth himself in some pit or gaping of the earth, vntill that sunny heat be abated. . . . The fourth and fift kinds . . . haue short necks, broad shoulders, rough Legs and feet, and small snouts, and little eies: herein they differ one kind from another, because that one of them hath a backe of a silver colour, and a white belly, and the lower part of the feet blacks and this is Ictinus canus, a gray Kite-wolfe: the other is black, hauing a lesser body, his haire standing continuously vpright, and liveth by hunting of Hares.

EDWARD TOPSELL,

THE HISTORIE OF FOUR-FOOTED BEASTES (1607)

Rabbits and Wolves

Long ago Rabbit and his wife, Frog, were talking. Rabbit said, "I saw a windigo on the trail a little while ago." Frog said, "We should go kill it."

They followed the windigo's trail and found the windigo in the shape of a moose. Frog said, "Go kill the windigo." But Rabbit said, "I'm afraid."

Frog attacked the windigo. She jumped into its rectum and crawled through its body. Then she bit its heart. The windigo died. Then Frog got out of the moose's corpse.

Frog and Rabbit started eating the moose. Then a pack of wolves came along. Frog jumped into a hole, but Rabbit decided to stay and eat more.

The wolves jumped on the moose carcass and ate it up. Because Rabbit was stupid, they ate him too. So it is today that wolves chase rabbits all the time.

SANDY LAKE CREE FOLKTALE

Resurrection

We can try and kill all that is native, string it up by its hind legs for all to see, but spirit howls and wildness endures.

TERRY TEMPEST WILLIAMS

Iranian Wolves

Every winter the two major Teheran newspapers published grisly accounts of people being attacked by wolves, some of which reputedly occurred in the northwestern part of the country. As well as following up on reported livestock losses in Arasbaran, I also investigated possible attacks on humans. Most reports involved villagers traveling alone who, upon seeing a wolf pack for the first time in their lives, had fled believing they had escaped from a wolf attack. This was in contrast to shepherds, who saw wolves frequently and were not afraid of them.

I followed up on the only report of a shepherd having been attacked and supposedly killed by wolves. Eventually, I located a shepherd who had witnessed the man's death. Both had been attending a flock of sheep when about a dozen wolves appeared. One shepherd worked at bunching the flock while the other, with the aid of three dogs, attempted to drive off the wolves. The dogs pulled down one wolf and the shepherd clubbed it to death with his cane. Meanwhile, a boy who also witnessed the attack ran for help. Several men from the local village arrived and helped drive the remaining wolves off. At this point, the shepherd with the dogs sat down, coughed and died. The cause of his death was unknown, but it certainly was not a wolf kill.

PAUL JOSLIN (1982)

The Wrestler

It was the custom of the Arcadians to shed human blood in their solemn sacrifice to Lycaean Zeus. Once upon a time a certain Daemoetas of Parrhasia tasted the entrails of a child who had been slain for sacrifice and immediately turned into a wolf. Ten years later the same man regained his human form and won the wrestlers' prize at the Olympic games.

AGRIOPAS, *OLYMPIONICAE* (CA. 150 B.C.)

Lived-with-Wolves

At one time the People spoke the same language as the animals. They often intermarried, and the separation between people and other creatures became less and less distinct. At that time Lived-with-Wolves stayed in the home of his grandmother. Each spring she took him to a rock pinnacle and had him wait atop it while she went off for one or two weeks at a time. Always when she returned she was pregnant with a litter of cubs that she raised as his sisters and brothers. Lived-with-Wolves wondered about this, so he followed her and saw her copulating with a wolf. When he saw this the magical bond between people and animals was broken, and they lived apart from each other from that time on.

CHIPEWYAN LEGEND

Woman Who Lived with Wolves

O nce, in deepest winter, a woman fought with her husband and ran away from their camp. After four days she had no more food left, and she became weak and fatigued.

She came to a hill and found a cave. She crawled inside and lay down. When she awoke, she found herself among a pack of wolves. The biggest of them said, "Don't worry. We are your friends. We will not hurt you." They fed her on deer meat.

She lived with them for two years. The wolves hunted and brought her meat, and she made pemmican for them. She tanned the hides for herself.

Then the wolf chief said, "It is time for you to return to your people." He told the woman to follow a herd of wild horses for two days, and they would lead her to a place near her former camp. He said that the stallion might try to keep her, but that she should run away from him if he did.

The woman left, but remained with the horses for two years. Her people came upon the herd one day and captured it, the woman included. When they found her among the horses, her relatives took care of her. They did not return her to her husband, but it was a long time before she behaved like a human again. Her people called her "Woman Who Lived with Wolves." Other people called her "Cave Woman."

TETON SIOUX FOLKTALE

Howl

The wolf's howl never fails to affect me personally with a peculiar prickling in the scalp that I doubt not is a racial inheritance from the Stone Age.

ERNEST THOMPSON SETON, *THE ARCTIC PRAIRIES* (1911)

Call of the Wild

And now loud-howling wolves arouse the jades
That drag the tragic melancholy night. . .

WILLIAM SHAKESPEARE,

THE SECOND PART OF KING HENRY VI, ACT 4, SC. 1 (1588)

The Boy and the Wolves

Deep in a forest lived a hunter and his wife and children. They stayed far from their tribesmen, who were cruel and deceitful. The hunter and his family lived in the forests for many years until one day disease came to their lodge, and the hunter sickened. He called to his wife and said, "You will not be long in joining me in the spirit world. You will not suffer." Then he called to his children and said, "You are young. You will have to endure much evil in the world. Promise to love each other and take care of your younger brother. Do not return to the tribe." Then he died. Soon thereafter his wife died too.

The older brother said to the sister, "I am going to see our tribesmen." She went to find him not long afterward, leaving the younger brother behind with a store of food. She found the older brother living happily in a large village, and she remained there.

The younger brother went into the woods when the store of food was gone. He ate roots and berries until deep winter set in. Then he came upon a pack of wolves and joined them in their meals. They always made sure he had enough to eat.

When the winter came and the lakes thawed, the older brother went out hunting. He heard his younger brother singing to him: "Brother, I am becoming a wolf!" Then the younger brother howled long and low and turned into a wolf.

The older brother returned to the village and told his sister what had happened. For the rest of their lives they mourned for their brother, whom they had abandoned.

CHUKCHEE FOLKTALE

Wolf's Lashes

There once was a blacksmith who had an only child, Akiko, a daughter. His wife had died in childbirth, and he took as his new wife an ill-tempered, demanding woman who worked Akiko to the bone throughout her youth. For all that, Akiko remained a kind young woman. She gave her father's workers the small wages she received, and they in turn worked so hard that the blacksmith soon became wealthy.

The stepmother began to tell Akiko's father that his daughter was a woman of easy virtue. "She gives away your fortune to those laggards," she said. Angered, the blacksmith ordered his daughter to leave his house.

Dejected, Akiko walked into the snowy mountains. "Many wolves live there," she thought. "They will eat me and take away my cares." She called out to the trees, "Wolf, wolf, come kill me! I have no reason to live."

The branches parted in the nearby undergrowth, and there stood a huge wolf. It spoke to her in a human voice, saying, "Do not be afraid, Akiko. I won't kill you. I do not harm people—that is, if they really are people, as you are. You can't recognize real people, I fear. You place too much trust in everyone. But this will help you." He plucked out a pair of his eyelashes and handed them to Akiko, saying, "When you want to know who you're dealing with, look through these eyelashes. Trust only those whose features do not change."

Akiko went on through the mountains to the nearest village. She was startled to see that its inhabitants had strange features indeed. One woman had the head of a chicken, pecking greedily at everything in sight. Another had the head of a fish. An administrator had a fat pig's face, and the household servants had the appearance of mice and small birds. Only one person, a young charcoal-maker, kept his human form when she looked at him through the wolf's eyelashes.

She approached him at his hut that night. At first he said, "Go away, ghost. Do not do me evil."

Akiko assured him that she was not a ghost and told him her story. Then she asked for a drink of water. The charcoal-maker pointed to a shallow well nearby.

Akiko went to the well and saw, glistening under the water's surface, a huge chunk of gold. The water tasted like the finest *sake*. She took it and returned to the charcoal-maker's hut, saying, "We can take this gold and exchange it for money. Then we can build an inn around the *sake* well." They named the inn "The Old Charcoal Pile" and amassed a fortune there, all thanks to the kind wolf's intercession.

JAPANESE FOLKTALE

Twilight of the Gods

The gods captured Loki, dragged him without pity into his cavern. They captured his children, Vali and Nari, and changed Vali into a wolf. The wolf then tore Nari limb from limb. Then the gods bound Loki to the cave by his own entrails, and atop him placed a serpent, whose venom drips on him and causes him to twist and howl so violently that the earth shakes. Loki and Vali will be there until Ragnarok, the twilight of the gods.

Then will come the winter, called Fimbull-winter, during which snow will fall from the four corners of the world. . . . Brothers, for the sake of mere gain, shall kill each other, and sisters' children will rend their kinship ties. Hard and wanton will be the age. An ax-age, a sword-age, shields broken in two, a storm-age, a wolf-age, before the earth shall meet her doom.

The wolf will devour the sun, and a great loss that will be to humankind. The wolf will devour the moon, and a great loss will that be as well. Then the stars will shoot out of the heavens, and the forests will be uprooted, and the mountains will fall from their foundations, and the world will come to an end.

OLD NORSE LEGEND

Wolves and Witches

In some countries they nail a woolves head to the door . . . to prevent and cure all mischeefes wrought by charmes and witchcraftes. . . . They hang *Scila* (which is either a roote, or rather in this place garlike) in the roofe of the house, for to keep awaie witches and spirits: and so they do Alicium also.

REGINALD SCOT,
THE DISCOVERIE OF WITCHCRAFT (1665)

Big Wolf

He goes out to hunt
Big Wolf I am
With his black bow he goes out to hunt
With his feathered arrows he goes out to hunt
Big Wolf I am
I shoot the big male game through the shoulder
It obeys me in death

NAVAJO WOLFWAY CEREMONIAL

Man's Fate

If all the beasts were gone, man would die from loneliness of spirit, for whatever happens to the beast happens to the man.

CHIEF SEATTLE

Benedictio

Even if in these late days the old gods, Chief Wolf, Chief Bear, and others, no longer come and talk with us in person, we know that they still roam the earth, that they live in some far part of it which the white men have not yet found and desecrated, and we have the assurance that they still visit us in the spirit, unseen and unheard except as they appear to us in our dreams. And we know that they still heed our prayers and intercede for us with the sun, ruler of all, for his mercy and aid.

MORNING EAGLE, BLACKFOOT SHAMAN (CA. 1880)

Sheep, Wolf, and Hare

Once there lived an old sheep. Every summer she and her lamb would climb up into the northern plateau to graze. One day, as they traveled, the two came upon a ferocious-looking wolf.

"Good morning, Auntie Sheep," said the wolf. "Where are you going?"

"Oh, wolf, to pasture! We're doing no harm!"

"Well," the wolf said. "All the same, I'm hungry."

The sheep said, "If you wait until fall we'll both be fat. Eat us on our way back home."

The wolf thought about this for a while and then consented. The sheep and lamb grazed throughout the summer and then made their way southward. As they approached the wolf's place they became very sad. A hare, hopping about nearby, came over and asked them why they looked so downcast.

They told him the story, and the hare promised to protect them. He produced a pen, some ink, and a piece of parchment, and then jumped on the sheep's back. In this way the hare rode down to where the wolf stood. When they arrived the hare challenged him, saying, "Who are you? What are you doing?"

The wolf replied, "I am a wolf. We arranged this meeting earlier. Who are you?"

The hare replied, "I am a hare. I am on my way to India by appointment to the Emperor. I have been ordered to bring ten wolf skins to the Emperor of India as a present. What good luck that I've found you!" He then took the parchment and made a large number 1.

The wolf fled from the authority of the Emperor, and the sheep continued happily homeward.

TIBETAN FOLKTALE

El Lobo

The dread of this great wolf spread yearly long the ranchmen, and each year a larger price was set on his head, until at last it reached $1,000, an unparalleled wolf-bounty, surely; many a good man has been hunted down for less. Tempted by the promised reward, a Texan ranger named Tannerey came one day galloping up the cañon of the Currumpaw. He had a superb outfit for wolf-hunting—the best of guns and horses, and a pack of enormous wolf-hounds. Far out on the plains of the Pan-handle, he and his dogs had killed many a wolf, and now he never doubted that, within a few days, Old Lobo's scalp would dangle at his saddle-bow.

Away they went bravely on their hunt in the gray dawn of a summer morning, and soon the great dogs gave joyous tongue to say that they were already on the track of their quarry. Within two miles, the grizzly band of Currumpaw leaped into view, and the chase grew fast and furious. The part of the wolf-hounds was merely to hold the wolves at bay till the hunter could ride up and shoot them, and this usually was easy on the open plains of Texas, but here a new feature of the country came into play, and showed how well Lobo had chosen his range; for the rocky cañons of the Currumpaw and its tributaries intersect the prairies in every direction. The old wolf at once made for the nearest of these and by crossing it got rid of the horseman. His band then scattered and thereby scattered the dogs, and when they reunited at a distant point of course all of the dogs did not turn up, and the wolves no longer outnumbered, turned on their pursuers and killed or desperately wounded them all. That night when Tannerey mustered his dogs, only six of them returned, and of these, two were terribly lacerated. This hunter made two other attempts to capture the royal scalp, but neither of them was more successful than the first, and on the last occasion his best horse met its death by a fall; so he gave up the chase in disgust and went back to Texas, leaving Lobo more than ever the despot of the region.

Next year, two other hunters appeared, determined to win the promised bounty. Each believed he could destroy this noted wolf, the first by means of a newly devised poison, which was to be laid out in an entire new manner; the other a French Canadian, by poison assisted with certain spells and charms, for he firmly believed that Lobo was a veritable "loup-garou," and could not be killed by ordinary means. But cunningly compounded poisons, charms, and incantations were all of no avail against this grizzly devastator. He made his weekly rounds and daily banquets as aforetime, and before many weeks had passed, Calone and Laloche gave up in despair and went elsewhere to hunt.

In the spring of 1893, after his unsuccessful attempt to capture Lobo, Joe Calone had a humiliating experience, which seems to show that the big wolf simply scorned his enemies, and had absolute confidence in himself. Calone's farm was on a small tributary of the Currumpaw, in a picturesque cañon, and among the rocks of this very cañon, within a thousand yards of the house, Old Lobo and his mate selected their den and raised their family that season. There they lived all summer, and killed Joe's cattle, sheep, and dogs, but laughed at all his poisons and traps, and rested securely among the recesses of the cavernous cliffs, while Joe vainly racked his brain for some method of smoking them out, or of reaching them with dynamite. But they escaped entirely unscathed, and continued their ravages as before. "There's where he lived all last summer," said Joe, pointing to the face of the cliff, "and I couldn't do a thing with him. I was like a fool to him."

ERNEST THOMPSON SETON, *WILD ANIMALS I HAVE KNOWN* (1898)

Wolf and Fox

O nce upon a time a wolf and a fox shared a den. The wolf, being stronger, ordered the fox to do his work for him. The fox, for his part, plotted to get rid of the wolf somehow.

One day they were out walking, when the wolf said, "Fox, find me something to eat or I'll eat you!"

"Well," said the fox, "I know a farmyard where there are two yearling lambs. Let's go steal one." The fox stole one and brought it to the wolf. The wolf ate the lamb but still was hungry. He went to get the other yearling, but he shambled about in the farmyard so loudly that the lamb and its dam bleated in alarm, bringing the farmers down on him. They beat him with sticks. The wolf finally ran off.

"You led me into a trap," he said to the fox. "The farmers nearly did me in!"

"Why not be satisfied with a smaller meal?" asked the fox.

The next day the wolf said, "Fox, find me something to eat or I'll eat you!"

The fox said, "I know a farmhouse where the wife always makes pancakes. Let's go steal some." They went there, and the fox stole a stack of pancakes and took them to the wolf.

"Now you've got lots to eat," the fox said. But the wolf ate the pancakes in a single bite and said, "I'm still hungry." The wolf went to the farm and tried to run off with the entire plate of pancakes. He dropped

Fox and Wolf Go Fishing

the plate, which shattered. The farmer's wife heard the racket and called her husband and field hands. They beat the wolf until he ran.

The wolf said to the fox, "You led me into a trap again!"

Again the fox asked him, "Why not be satisfied with a smaller meal?"

The next day the wolf said, "Fox, find me something to eat or I'll eat you!"

The fox replied, "Well, I know where a man has been salting beef. Let's go steal some."

"This time," the wolf said, "I'm going with you so that you can help me escape if we get into trouble." The fox led him to the man's salting cellar. They found whole sides of beef there. The wolf immediately gobbled down as much as he could hold. The fox ate sparingly, looking around alertly.

The man came into the cellar. The fox jumped out the hole through which he and the wolf had entered. The wolf ran there too, but he had eaten so much that he could not fit through it. The man clubbed him to death, while the fox snickered over the fate of the gluttonous wolf.

SILESIAN FOLKTALE

O nce there were a wolf and a fox.

The wolf said to the fox, "Friend, let's go steal a lamb and share it."

"Yes, let's," said the fox.

They went to a sheep fold and stole a lamb.

Then the fox said, "One lamb won't be enough. Let's go fishing too."

"All right," said the wolf. "We'll need a rod and line, though."

The fox said, "You're strong. Take that big pot for a float. I'll use this gourd. When we're finished, we'll eat. Let's hide the lamb behind these reeds."

"All right," said the wolf.

They hid the lamb by the shore. The fox tied the heavy pot to the wolf's neck, and the dry gourd to his own waist, and they went into the sea and fished.

The wolf called out, "I've caught a fish."

The fox said, "It's too small. You'll have to go farther out to get the big ones."

The wolf swam out farther. The pot filled with water and the trusting wolf drowned. Trickster fox returned to his lair and devoured the lamb by himself.

MODERN GREEK FOLKTALE

142

Wolf Brother

When Manabozho [the Menomini culture hero] had accomplished the works for which Kisha' Ma'nido sent him down to the earth, he went far away and built his wigwam on the northeastern shore of a large lake, where he took up his abode. Because he was alone, the good *manidos* gave him a brother, whom they brought to life and called Naq'pote. He was formed like a human being, but, being a *manido,* could assume the shape of a wolf, in which form he hunted for food. Manabozho was aware of the anger of the bad *manidos* who dwelt beneath the earth, and warned his brother, the Wolf, never to return home by crossing the lake, but always to go around along the shore. Once, after the Wolf had been hunting all day long, he found himself directly opposite his wigwam and, being tired, concluded to cross the lake. He had not gone halfway across when the ice broke, so the Wolf was seized by the bad *manidos,* and destroyed. Manabozho at once knew what had befallen his brother, and in his distress mourned for four days. Every time Manabozho sighed, the earth trembled, which caused the hills and ridges to form over its surface. Then the shade of Moquaio, the Wolf, appeared before Manabozho, and knowing that his brother could not be restored, Manabozho told him to follow the path of the setting sun and become the chief of the shades in the hereafter. Manabozho then hid himself in a large rock near Mackinaw. Here his uncles, the People, for many years visited Manabozho, and always built a long lodge, the *mitatwiko'mik,* where they sang; so when Manabozho did not wish to see them in his human form he appeared to them in the form of a little white rabbit, with trembling ears, just as he had first appeared to Nokomis.

MENOMINI LEGEND

Wolf Creates the World

Wolf, the strongest man in the world, paddled around in a canoe feeling lonely. He created Coyote and called him brother. Wolf decided that they should not spend eternity paddling around. They needed to create earth on which to live, so they each took a handful of dirt and put it on the water. They added more dirt to this earthen island. Coyote ran around and declared it to be too small to roam in, so Wolf added more dirt until Coyote was satisfied. That is how the world was created.

OWENS VALLEY PAIUTE LEGEND

Wolves Are Not Like Dogs

Wolves are not like dogs, you know. A dog father knows not his own children. A wolf marries and he and his wife live always together until death. When children come, he hunts for them, and brings food for them, and watches over them faithfully while the mother goes out to hunt and run around and keep up her strength. Ah, they are wise, true-hearted animals, the big wolves of the plains.

RED EAGLE, BLACKFOOT WARRIOR (CA. 1880)

The Silence of the Wolves

Tacitorum more luporum

Ore premunt voces

The wolf is characteristically silent.

OVID, METAMORPHOSES XIV, 778–79

Two Fables by Aesop

I. A wolf got the bone of a bird stuck in its throat and was in danger of dying. He asked a crane to put her head into his throat and remove the bone, promising to pay a large sum of money in return. The crane pulled the bone out and asked for his payment. The wolf grinned and said, "The way I see it, I've already paid you. After all, you're still alive."

II. A wolf passed by the door of a hut in which some shepherds sat gorging themselves on a roasted leg of lamb. The wolf said to them, "Think what you'd do if I behaved as you are doing now!"

The Wolf and the Soldier

There once was a wolf who lived near Fontaine-blanche. He had heard that no one could compete with the animal called man.

One day the wolf followed the road to Areney. When he reached the Croixcassé he met an old woman. The wolf halted and told her what he had heard. "I want to fight this animal called man," he declared.

The old woman said, "Go to Fontaine-blanche. Ask the soldier there if he wants to fight."

When the wolf came to Fontaine-blanche he found a soldier. The wolf halted. He said to the soldier, "Do you want to fight?"

The soldier said, "All right, if you want, we'll fight."

The wolf said, "Throw some dust in my eyes to enrage me."

The soldier loaded his musket. He said, "Stand back!" Then he shot the wolf square in the eyes.

"You spit an awful fire!" cried the wolf.

The wolf turned to run, and the soldier drew his sword and cut off the wolf's thigh. Later another wolf saw the wolf limping and asked him, "What happened?"

"I wanted to fight an animal called man. He spat in my face and hit me with a stick."

"Well," the other wolf replied, "you should have kept it to yourself."

FRENCH FOLKTALE

House of the Wolves

Ha-Sass, planning with his brothers how he could gain entrance to the House of the Wolves, decided he would drain his blood out, so they could not scent him as man. Finding a large flat stone on the beach, covered with barnacles, he lay down upon it and had his brothers pull him against the barnacles—four times, once on each side of his body, and his arms as well. He was bleeding all over, and finally, when enough blood had been let, he had his brothers sew him into the skin of a hair seal. They knew the Wolves ate the hair seal; so, after sewing Ha-Sass inside the skin, the brothers carried him on a flat piece of wood over to the beach. Ha-Sass kept a small flat stone close upon his chest because he knew that when the Wolves had a dead thing, they would try to catch it on a sharp stick to make sure it was dead. Raven, messenger of the Wolves, saw the hair seal on the beach and, flying over, took out its right eye as a sign to the Wolves that Raven had been there. Raven does this with everything he finds on the beach: hair seal, sea lion, or whatnot. Ha-Sass's brothers were

watching, to see which way Raven went. He flew right up the mountain, but his house was not in the Wolves' House. Then the brothers saw many Wolves come down to the beach. These took up the hair seal, and all went away into the bush. The largest of the Wolves is the Carrier Wolf. There is only one of these to each pack, and his back is different—wider, for carrying things so they will not fall off. The others merely go along with him to help. It was the Carrier Wolf who took Ha-Sass in the hair seal skin upon his back, and after a time he said, "This creature feels warm. It must be alive. There must be a man alive in it." Carrier Wolf, who is the main helper of the Wolf Chief, is also wiser than the common Wolves, and at this point the Carrier threw Ha-Sass from his back against the sharp sticks that lined the whole road to the Wolves' House, and against which they dash whatever they take, to make sure it has been killed. But the wary Ha-Sass was also watching, and, as he held the flat stone closely to his breast, he bounced off from these each time. Finally the Carrier Wolf took him on his back, and they went on

their way. They at last reached the secret fastness of the Wolves, very far up in the mountains, and entered the house of the Wolf Chief. All the Wolves had gone along; for they, together with the Carrier Wolf, worked for the Wolf Chief, and when they got any food must take it to him. When they all came together in the Wolf Chief's home, the Carrier at once complained that he was tired, as what he had been carrying was very heavy. As soon as the hair seal was inside the house, they started to cut it into pieces, so that the Wolves could eat right away and make a feast. They had gathered into a circle for this, and when the Wolf Chief cut into the skin they found the man alive inside. Then they began asking him questions, for the Wolf Chief, who was wise beyond all others, knew that he would not have undergone the dangers of coming up there unless he had desired something. Admiring his courage, they promised him anything he wished. . . . The Wolves first asked him if he would like something for catching whales, but he remained silent. Then they asked him if he wanted a comb, so he could have long hair, but again he did not answer. Next they asked him if he wanted *teksyah'pe,* something which, if placed inside a dead body, would bring it back to life. Again he did not answer. Finally the Wolves asked if he wanted the *che-to'kh,* and Ha-Sass at once replied that this was what he wanted. The *che-to'kh* was a magic club that, held high, caused all who saw it to fall dead. It was never represented in carvings because people died when they saw it. Ha-Sass too died when he first saw it, but the Wolves brought him back to life again by putting *teksyah'pe* upon his body. They brought him back to life four times.

NOOTKA LEGEND

Wolf and Dog

An old woman was once digging roots; she had taken her dog along. A wolf came from the opposite direction. The dog ran up towards the wolf. "Don't come here, why are you coming here? You envy me because my owner always goes around with me." The wolf said, "What have I got to envy you for? Your owner beats you. When your owner has food hidden in camp and you take it they hit you over the head with a club." The dog said, "What of it? I have meat to steal and I'll steal it, but you have nothing." The wolf replied, "I can eat anything I want. There is no one to bother or hit me. You are blistered from tail to head with beatings." The dog asked, "What good things do you eat? When men kill buffalo, you are afraid to come there till they have gone, and you merely get the leavings. When men are butchering you'll sit down at a distance, afraid to eat. Your armpits stink, and you straighten out the hair there with your teeth." The wolf answered, "You have nothing to say about me, snotnose." The dog said, "What do you have to say of me? When I get back to camp and men come, my owner always throws me something." The wolf answered, "Show me when you have enough to warm your belly. When your owners are going out to ease themselves, you follow them to eat their droppings." The old woman had her digging-stick resting against her breast; she was leaning on the handle and listening. "Go away," the wolf said. "We'll fight for as long as we want to."

CROW FOLKTALE

CAPTIONS

To identify illustrations, refer to these caption page numbers as you leaf through this book on the lives of wolves.

▲ DENOTES DIGITAL ILLUSTRATION

REFERENCES

Barker, W. H. *West African Folk-Tales*. London: Harrap, 1895.

Barnouw, Victor. *Wisconsin Chippewa Myths and Tales*. Madison: University of Wisconsin Press, 1977.

Boas, Franz. *The Mythology of the Bella Coola Indians*. New York: American Museum of Natural History, 1898.

Borogas, Waldemar. *The Eskimo of Siberia*. New York: American Museum of Natural History, 1913.

Borogas, Waldemar. *Tales of the Yukaghir, Lamut, and Russianized Natives of Siberia*. New York: American Museum of Natural History, 1918.

Budge, Wallace. *Egyptian Tales*. London: T. Butterworth, 1921.

Dorsey, James Owen. *A Study of Souian Cults*. Washington, D.C.: Bureau of American Ethnology, 1894.

Emerson, Ellen Russell. *Indian Myths*. n.p., 1887.

Goodwin, Grenville. *Myths and Tales of the White Mountain Apache*. New York: American Folklore Society, 1937.

Grattan, J. H. G., and C. Singer. *Anglo-Saxon Magic and Medicine*. Oxford: Oxford University Press, 1952.

Keefe, James, and Lynn Morrow, eds. *The White River Chronicles of S. C. Turnbo*. Fayetteville: University of Arkansas Press, 1994.

Littman, Enno. *Publications of the Princeton Expedition to Abyssinia*. Leyden: E. J. Brill, 1910.

Lowie, Robert H. *Myths and Traditions of the Crow Indians*. New York: American Museum of Natural History, 1918.

Matthews, Washington. *Navaho Folk-Tales*. Washington, D.C.: Bureau of American Ethnology, 1886.

Novak, Miroslav. *Folktales from Japan*. London: Hamlyn, 1970.

O'Connor, W. F. *Folk Tales from Tibet*. London: Hurst and Blackett, 1906.

Owen, Mary Alicia. *Folklore of the Musquakie Indians of North America*. Toronto: The Folk-Lore Society, 1902.

Philippi, Donald L. *Songs of Gods, Songs of Humans*. Tokyo: University of Tokyo Press, 1979.

Rexroth, Kenneth. *Collected Shorter Poems*. New York: New Directions, 1966.

Roosevelt, Theodore, and George Bird Grinnell, eds. *Hunting in Many Lands*. New York: Forest and Stream Publishing, 1895.

Sian-Tek, Lim. *More Folktales from China*. New York: John Day Company, 1948.

Tantaquidgeon, Gladys. *A Study of Delaware Indian Medicine Practice and Folk Beliefs*. Harrisburg: Pennsylvania Historical Commission, 1942.

Walker, J. R. *The Sun Dance and Other Ceremonies of the Teton Dakota*. New York: American Museum of Natural History, 1917.

Wissler, Clark. *Societies and Ceremonial Associations in the Oglala Division of the Teton-Dakota*. New York: American Museum of Natural History, 1912.

Wood-Martin, W. G. *Traces of the Elder Faiths of Ireland*. London: Longmans, Green, and Co., 1902.

Classical Latin and Greek texts are translated from the definitive Loeb Classical Library and Oxford Classical Texts editions. German folktales are translated from Jacob and Wilhelm Grimm's *Hausmärchen* (1851) and R. Büchthold and W. Staübli's *Handwörterbuch des Deutschen Aberglaubens* (1927–1942).

ACKNOWLEDGMENTS

To the dynamic five of Art Wolfe, Inc.—whose negotiating, editing, arranging, and meticulous review of material has been my greatest support and security for developing projects such as this book—I offer my sincere appreciation to Mel Calvan, Christine Eckhoff, Gavriel Jecan, Ray Pfortner, and Deirdre Skillman. Special thanks are due to Brandt Aymar, who led me to Greg McNamee. I am grateful for the opportunity Brandt made available and for all the assistance he provided along the way. Also of Crown Publishers, Patty Eddy deserves great credit for her friendly guidance in the world of commercial publishing and Lauren Dong for so patiently working with our design concerns. In addition, I received the help and support of many others whose talents and expertise made my work possible. I give my thanks to all those mentioned here: Ken Kehrer, Denali National Park; Gary Stolz, U.S. Department of the Interior; Jenny Ryan; Tom Buffington; Eric Shallit; Terry Caleen; Ford Gilbreth; Sara Herrett; Kay Bartlett; Sue Behrens; and the Point Defiance Red Wolf Project.